DEDICATION

To Great Spirit, Father-Mother-God, I am blessed to be an emissary of light and one of the many earth volunteers who chose to come to this planet to forget my Oneness and go through all the cycles of life. As my veils of forgetfulness have been lifted, I have reawakened to my true divinity and am now dedicated to serving Mother Gaia and humanity in the ascension process.

I dedicate this book to all the teachers and guides both from heaven and on earth who have supported me on this path of enlightenment as I return back to Sacred Union.

This book is also dedicated to the spirit of the Blue Ridge Mountains in Asheville, North Carolina. As I was nearing completion of this book, during my sabbatical to Asheville, North Carolina, I received guidance that Goddess of Peace, the sacred wisdom teachings of Ascended Master Sarah, was a portal to awaken all others so they may return to peace and live in balance in Divine Holy Sacred Union with All That Is.

ACKNOWLEDGMENTS

My deepest gratitude to Ascended Master Sarah and the Holy Family who has blessed my life with their love and sacred wisdom. I am honored to be the oracle for Sarah's Sacred Wisdom Teachings.

Special Thanks to:
Tine Overton my Sarah Sis-Star, who assisted me in the original creation of the Sarah channeled teaching. I am grateful to you for your love and support!

Jared Willis and Beverly Oberline, thank you both for your willingness to transcribe Sarah's messages! Sarah's story would not have been able to be heard without your help! You are both my Earth Angels!

Other Acknowledgments:

Donna Kirby. and all my friends who supported me with this project.
Courtney Davis: original print cover design
Pam Daniel: Graphic Design
Pam Silver Eagle: Grail Light code photography
Susan Krusemark: Editing
Ruth Souther: Editing and CHI publishing service
I thank you all from the bottom of my heart!

Sacred Wisdom Teachings of Sarah, Goddess of Peace

Lea Chapin

CRYSTAL HEART
IMPRINTS

In an effort to present the information in the context in which it was received, material in this book may seem different from other spiritual books as it was dictated literally to the author. You may find important principles repeated for emphasis. We suggest that you read this book with an open mind and loving heart to attain the greatest level of understanding.

Courtney Davis: original print cover design
Pam Daniel: Graphic Design
Interior Layout: Ruth A. Souther
Editing: Ruth A. Souther
First Edition Printing 2022. Printed in the USA.
ISBN: 978-0-9762974-8-2
Spirituality and New Age
Published by Crystal Heart Imprints

Sacred Wisdom Teachings of Sarah, Goddess of Peace

CONTENTS

Chapter 1	Sarah: She Who Is the Missing Holy Grail	Pg 3
Chapter 2	Yeshua Shares Sarah's Sacred Soul Mission	Pg 9
Chapter 3	In Search of the Holy Grail	Pg 17
Chapter 4	Sarah, the Nurturer and Awakener of Divine Cosmic Love, Peace and Grace	Pg 25
Chapter 5	Sarah, Torchbearer of Divine Sacred Union	Pg 31
Chapter 6	Rebirthing Into Oneness In the Cave of Creation	Pg 37
Chapter 7.	Reconnecting With Mother Gaia to Return to Love	Pg 45
Chapter 8	The Power of Divine Sophia to Heal the Wounds of the Sacred Feminine	Pg 53
Chapter 9	Rebirthing the Old Patriarchal Rule of Fear and Separation	Pg 59
Chapter 10	Opening Your Heart to Divine Mother Love	Pg 65
Chapter 11	Stepping Into Your Still Point to Remember Your Divine Self	Pg 71
Chapter 12	Infusing the New Grail Light Codes Onto the Planet	Pg 77
Chapter 13	Invoking the Diamond Light to Return to Sacred Union	Pg 83
Chapter 14	Sarah Anchors Integration of Divine Union Within Your Being	Pg 91
Chapter 15	Return to Sacred Divine Union	Pg 97
12 Tools	Narrated by Mary Magdalene	Pg 105
12 Tools	Narrated by Yeshua (Jesus the Christ)	Pg 107

Testimonial

"Lea brings forth a profound work of channeling on ushering in the New Age, one of Light and radical transformation through the voice of Master Sarah. The emphasis on Unity and Balance between two equal poles - the Masculine and the Feminine - is heavily emphasized and the impending blessings - should One choose to receive - revealed.

It is also a message of Hope and persevering in any time that brings us new - or old - challenges. This new book is a wonderful gift to those who embody the Light frequency of the planet, our holy Mother Earth. We can find strength in our guides, our sacred mission, knowing that we are never alone and working for a higher purpose in the Ultimate Presence of the Divine."

Maxime Lichtenberg
Writer, Poetess & Red Tent Healer
www.maxilichtenberg.com
@maximelichtenberg Instagram

Testimonial

Sacred Wisdom teaching of Sarah, Goddess of Peace, reminds us that what we are searching for is inside of ourselves if we have the courage to look deep within our own souls! Inner Peace can be a reality! Simply breathe and let go!

Sarah teaches us that we have the power to change the world if we believe! Imagine a world filled with peace! It begins with you! Let your light shine so others may see! Sarah's Sacred wisdom teachings is a must read for all who wish to be at peace!

Joanne Weiland
Founder. Link to Expert
www.linktoexpert.com

Testimonial

Lea's channeled book shows the true beauty of Sarah's mission here on Earth - which is only just now being brought to the consciousness of humankind, and allows the reader, through Divine Grace to receive frequencies of Divine Light needed at this time. An incredible gift to all of us who are ready to hear Sarah's call!" Rachel Goodwin, Author of 'Weaving the Strands of Sarayei—channeled wisdom from the Ascended Master Sarah.

Rachel Goodwin
connecting soul and spirit
Ph: (0045) 23937338
www.rachelgoodwin.dk/

Preface

As Ascended Master Sarah, I bring forth the return of the Divine Feminine into her rightful power. The Divine Feminine is reawakening to rebalance the misguided patriarchal rule that has controlled the planet for far too long. Your current civilization is at a crossroads and could no longer support the old patriarchal system that has controlled the world.

As a species, you are spiritually awakening at a very rapid rate and are rebalancing the feminine and masculine energies into a more balanced and harmonious state. Every soul has the opportunity to help birth the new consciousness on earth by honoring the Divine Feminine.

It is not about denying the value of the Divine Masculine but honoring both the yin and the yang aspects of one's spirit. The shift of consciousness is about restoring the Divine Feminine into her rightful place and position as the Divine Mother of Love, allowing her to be honored both for her leadership and from living from the heart.

Then the Divine Masculine can protect, strengthen, honor and serve the Sacred Feminine rather than being in competition with her in a way that no longer supports human spiritual evolution. It takes a lot of courage to walk the path of Sacred Union.

The old patriarchal rule of dominance and control are falling away. Those who hold wisdom, insight and love within their hearts are here to embrace change, as they are the pioneers of consciousness for birthing the new earth of love, peace, balance, and harmony, so peace shall prevail upon the planet.

There are many enlightened souls at the forefront of this shift of consciousness that are new earth beings. You have been drawn to this book because perhaps you are one of these souls. May you receive my wisdom teachings with an open heart so that you may be the change you wish to see, so peace and love may return to beloved Mother Gaia.

Blessings of love, light and peace to all.

Ascended Master Sarah

Chapter 1

Sarah:
She Who Is the Missing Holy Grail

Greetings, it is I, Sarah, the Daughter of Mary Magdalene and Yeshua ben Joseph. It is my honor to be the oracle for my parents as I bring forth the continuation of their love story and sacred soul mission. I am the representation of the missing chalice from the Last Supper that so many are seeking.

I come in your current civilization to reveal the truth of my parents' love story. My identity has been hidden for over 2,000 years as humanity was not able to accept or understand that my parents were Twin Flames who married and had children. I am privileged to be their firstborn and I carry the bloodline of their Divine Holy Sacred Union.

As the missing Holy Grail, I am carrying the bloodline for future generations to embody the essence of the Divine Feminine and Masculine energies that my parents held within their essence. My sacred soul contract is to bring balance to the earth so all humanity can reawaken to their true spiritual divinity and return to Divine Sacred Union within themselves.

As part of my sacred soul mission, I am bringing forth a powerful new flame upon the earth at this time. It is known as the Pearlescent White Flame of purity, love and innocence, as it is the spark of God's living light and love. As I was created in Sacred Union, I embody the essence of this powerful Pearlescent White Flame for it to be etched upon the earth and within the hearts of all souls.

This powerful flame's main activity is to unite the energy of the Sacred Masculine and Sacred Feminine energies into spiritual alchemy. The primary purpose of the flame is to create harmony, peace and balance upon the earth and into all souls. This flame represents the purity and innocence of God's love for all of humanity and all of creation.

Today, as you allow me to share my energy with you I ask that you invoke the Pearlescent White Flame within your essence. This flame of purity and innocence shall remain on the earth plane as a powerful resurrection flame for the next 2,000 years. As you invoke this flame it will help purify the lower vibrational frequencies of fear, anger and chaos that have kept you separate from God.

I now bring forth this beautiful flame to help humanity be at peace. Just as my parents brought forth their gift of love and peace to humanity, I am here to assist all souls to return to love and to be at peace.

As told in <u>Divine Union: The Love Story of Jesus and Mary Magdalene</u>, in my parents' lifetime, they both struggled to find harmony and balance within themselves. As powerful Ascended Masters, they were able to achieve their life lessons and unite and partner in Divine Holy

Sacred Union with their I Am presence. It was my parents' mission to help restore balance between the male and female polarities that have been held within humanity's collective consciousness.

It is why they were able to bring forth the beautiful template of their love of Divine Holy Sacred Union as an example unto others. My mother and father knew that their teachings would fall upon many deaf ears, which is why I, Sarah, have come as their voice to bring their teachings of Divine Holy Sacred Union once again upon the planet.

I am privileged to be their oracle to help awaken humanity to restore balance between the male and female distortions that are so prevalent on earth at this time. Unless humanity can balance the masculine and feminine expression of power in the world, the long-awaited Golden Age of Enlightenment cannot fully manifest upon the planet.

As I have stated, this is why I have made my presence known in order to help restore peace and balance upon Mother Earth. It is unfortunate that so many souls are lost and are unable to find peace within their own lives as they feel separate from their own I Am presence and Divine Self. This is why I am bringing the Pearlescent White Flame to help as many souls as possible to be at peace.

It is my mission to spark the energy of Divine Holy Sacred Union within one's essence so that all may return to balance as physical spiritual beings of light, living in joy and remembrance of who they truly are.

You, dear ones, are the new earth beings helping the earth in her ascension process into the fifth dimensional frequency. As lightworkers, you are all awakening and ascending into higher consciousness with Mother Gaia as well, for the planet is in need of your love, light and peace. I wish to help you integrate the vibrational frequency of the Pearlescent White Flame into your being so that you may merge in consciousness with your I Am presence.

I ask you to breathe in the frequency of this flame in its purest form, as you to return to Divine Holy Sacred Union. Dear ones, I understand the soul's journey can be most difficult, but please allow me to assist you through my sacred teachings. Please open your heart and feel the essence of the Pearlescent White Flame that I am bringing forth unto you at this time.

Can you feel the energy within your heart? Can you feel the energy of love as I bring the Pearlescent White Flame into your being? As you continue to open your heart to receive, I ask that you listen to the still quiet voice from within, which is your own innate wisdom.

My flame will help you to access a greater sense of clarity, peace and calm as you reawaken to the truth and the remembrance of who you truly are. May you accept my gift that I bring to you upon this day as I share my wisdom teachings of purity, love and innocence. I ask you to receive them with an open heart and open mind and allow my sacred teachings to live in your beautiful soul.

Go now, my children, and prepare yourselves to receive, as I help you to find the missing piece inside yourself that you have been seeking and searching for so long. May you be at peace. May you be at peace. May you be at peace. And so it is.

Ascended Master Sarah

Lea Chapin

Chapter 2

Yeshua Shares Sarah's Sacred Soul Mission

Greetings, it is I, Yeshua. It is my honor to share with you my daughter's sacred soul mission as she is known as the missing Holy Grail for she embodies the enlightened Christ/Magdalene energy of Divine Holy Sacred Union. As an enlightened avatar, she carries the Holy Grail light codes for the new earth energies to emerge in the Seventh Golden Age of Enlightenment.

She is here to awaken humanity as new earth beings living in Divine Holy Sacred Union with All That Is. She carries the sacred holy union of the divine spark of Oneness within all of creation. Her mission is to awaken all souls to live in joy and remembrance of who they truly are.

Sarah is an emissary of light as she is in advanced Ascended Master who has come to serve during this transformational period of global ascension. She will continue to serve humanity until all souls attain self-mastery. I come to share her story so she may be recognized for her sacred soul mission and her selfless service to humanity.

When Mary and I first became aware that my Mary was with child, we were very excited as we knew this special spirit would change the world. We realized that our child had a grand mission as she would continue the bloodline of our lineage. Mary and I were delighted to have a daughter and we named her Sarah, for in Hebrew, Sarah means "woman of high rank as a princess or noble woman."

We named her Elizabeth after my cousin, Elizabeth, and Mary's constant companion and confidant, Elizabeth. Elizabeth in Hebrew means, "bountiful God of plenty."

Elizabeth had indeed been a bountiful goddess of plenty for her generous spirit always overflowed with love, kindness, compassion, mercy. So we prayed that Sarah would carry these attributes as she carried Elizabeth's namesake as well.

Her formal name of Tamar was given to her for she was the original matriarch of the Holy House of Judea, and the name of King David's sister; therefore, we called her Sarah Elizabeth Tamar. She also is called by many other names as well, and in French she has been called Sara-La-Kali which means, "Sara the Black."

Sarah was born an advanced soul, fully awakened. When Sarah was born, we could not help but admire her because she was not only physically beautiful, but she had an inner beauty and an inner peace of divine radiance. As she grew into a young woman, her inner beauty was never overshadowed by her outer beauty for my daughter was one of the most sincere, kindest, and sweetest souls you will ever meet.

She was very thoughtful, had a loving and kind heart, and held great compassion for all those she met. Sarah had an innocence and purity of heart unlike any other. She was an untamed vessel of pure love and light.

Mary and I believed that this beautiful child that we created would one day heal many generations of souls throughout her lifetime and beyond. I was in awe of her magnificence as she held the sacred balance that Mary and I embodied. My daughter represents the missing Holy Grail which so many have been searching and seeking. Her mission is to continue the wisdom teachings of Mary's and my ministry.

Today, as I share the beautiful remembrance and the story of Sarah's life with you, may you feel the gift that she brings to the world. Sarah was born as a spiritually awakened being without her veil of forgetfulness. She did not have to struggle like Mary and I, as she was born with her own inner gnosis. She spoke at an early age and was wise beyond her years.

We knew that this tremendous soul was an enigma. Oftentimes, Mary and I would shake our heads in bewilderment; who was this child? Where did she come from? We were in awe of this grand master who chose to be our daughter.

Unlike Sarah, who was born with her own knowingness, Mary and I struggled with our own spiritual identities as we did not have the luxury of the veils of forgetfulness being removed at the time of our births. During the Age of Pisces, it was a difficult time period to be an awakened soul as humanity's consciousness was very heavy, dark and dense.

Sarah, however, was not overly affected by the weight

of these prevailing energies on the earth at that time, even though she was born an empath and felt the pain and suffering of others. As an empath, she felt the pain and suffering of the earth. She knew her sacred mission was to bring healing to Mother Gaia, in order for her to be restored back to her original state of grace.

It was difficult for her to feel the pain and suffering of Mother Earth for she loved her so. Mary and I tried to protect her as much as we could, but we trusted and knew that she had the ability to transmute her own pain and suffering as she was a powerful advanced Ascended Master.

Sarah's life was not always her own, but we knew her mission to assist in the healing of Mother Gaia and humanity was her great calling. Sarah had great inner strength and conviction and we knew that she would be able to master what she was called to do. Her love for Mother Earth and humanity is truly a great gift that Sarah brings to the world.

Dear ones, allow yourselves to receive my daughter's love for you so that you may be at peace. Sarah is a powerful soul for she is the blend of Mary's and my conjoined energies. Just like her mother, she is loving, kind and has an inner light that you can see radiating from her eyes.

Those who were honored to know her felt they were in the presence of a great master. Sarah's presence radiated compassion as her soul helped others to find love and to be at peace. As a pure soul, she was deeply committed to serving God and Mother Gaia. She is here today to continue with Mary's and my ministry as she holds our strength, our conviction to bring peace, love and forgiveness unto the world.

Sarah's gift to humanity is to assist the planet and humanity during these troubled times.

During Sarah's lifetime, I was amazed at how many souls she helped through her loving kindness and compassion. She often would share with me how she knew she had been a vessel to help others to love themselves and to be at peace. This gave her great comfort knowing that she was serving God and honoring her sacred soul contract.

May you open your hearts to Sarah's unconditional love and allow yourselves to feel her essence as she heals your soul. She is here to help awaken your soul to return to Oneness and live in joy and remembrance of who you truly are. Allow her to awaken your soul as she touches your heart.

Can you feel the warmth that Sarah is bringing unto you? Can you feel the essence of her love as she helps you to merge into Divine Holy Sacred Union with yourself?

Sarah has left many strands of her energy all over the world. Today, she is leaving a strand with you just as I speak. This is why she was honored and revered as Saint Sarah in St. Marie de la Mer in the Languedoc region of Southern France. When she arrived on the shore with her mother Mary and her aunts Mary Salome and Mary Jacob, she was disguised as a gypsy servant.

Her identity had to be hidden for their lives were in constant danger as they were hiding from the Romans after my crucifixion. As the gypsy servant, my Sarah was revered and honored by the gypsy/Roma people for her wisdom, knowledge, compassion, and love. She was recognized for the magnificent, loving, kind and wise soul that she was.

Perhaps this may surprise you, but Sarah is also the

representation of the Black Madonna. She is the image portrayed in the crypt of the church in St. Marie de la Mer. Saint Sarah, my daughter, is celebrated annually at the gypsy festival in May every year.

She is recognized as the patron saint of gypsies for the Roma people. That is why so many people are drawn to that region in Southern France for they are following the trail of Mary Magdalene and searching for the mysteries of the Holy Grail.

Many people are not aware of what they are truly searching for, for it is not the missing chalice but the search for the Sacred Union within themselves. Sarah embodies Divine Holy Sacred Union and is the physical embodiment of the missing chalice.

She is the divine spark of God that all are seeking inside of themselves. The intrigue of the missing Holy Grail in Southern France continues to this day, with the popularity of Dan Brown's book and movie, <u>The Da Vinci Code</u>. It has propelled much interest into that region of Southern France as the tourists continue to seek the mysteries and the story line of my Mary in that region.

Dear ones, part of that mystery is my daughter, Sarah, who holds the divine energy that all are seeking. She is here to teach love and to help humanity to honor themselves as sacred beings of light. She embodies love of such purity, strength and conviction that her desire to serve God is unstoppable.

As the perceived gypsy servant, she was known to be able to touch the hearts of so many by her gentle loving presence. Sarah's energy was innocent and pure, and it was with her purity that she was able to help others find love within themselves. May Sarah's teachings help you to find the inner love that you so long for. It is time to reconnect to my Sarah's energy as she helps you to reconnect to your true divinity.

You do not have to travel to Southern France to search for the clues of the missing grail for you are the piece that you are searching for, as all the secrets are inside of you. Open your heart and allow Sarah to help you to find the missing pieces that you have been searching for as you have been seeking reunification with your own spirit.

Sarah is known as the nurturer and awakener of cosmic love, peace and holy grace. When you call her name, you shall feel her strength, her love and her power. Sarah carries the vibration of a balanced ascended being as she is peace, love and light. She does not have to try to be anything because she just is. Mary and I marveled at her magnificence all of our lives. She embodied the divine as she was pure love.

Dear ones, remember that what you are searching for is truly inside of yourself. The missing grail is inside of you. Allow Sarah to help you to integrate into your Divine Self as she helps you to heal the shadow side of your humanness.

Perhaps this may surprise you but Sarah was able to help Mary and I to fully merge into partnership with ourselves and with one another. She was the catalyst and the nurturer-awakener, resurrecting our souls to help assist us to return to Divine Holy Sacred Union.

Dearest children, this is the gift that Sarah brings to you to help you to ascend and to return to Divine Union with yourselves. Sarah has come to be the reflection of your own soul as you move forward in your own ascension process.

Allow her to open your heart to Divine Union as she

assists you to return to union with your I Am presence. Go forth and allow my Sarah to assist you as you return to the Divine Union in which you were created.

May you be at peace. May you be at peace. May you be at peace. And so it is.

Ascended Master Yeshua

Chapter 3

In Search of the Holy Grail

Greetings, dear ones, it is I, Sarah. As I continue to share my mother's and father's love story I wish to help you understand who I am. As their firstborn child, I carried the bloodline of their Divine Holy Sacred Union. My parents were highly advanced adepts who were both trained in tantric sexual practices in the mystery schools of Egypt.

They were consciously taught how to bring forth the practice of light conception, to conceive children. This practice of consciously seeding children through ascension light codes is how I was conceived. As their child, I was born with very few veils of forgetfulness as I carried their bloodline of the Matri-Christ Grail lineage code.

As an advanced initiate carrying these light codes, I was born fully awakened in my own inner gnosis. As the guardian and activator of these Holy Grail ascension codes, I am known as the Awakener and Nurturer of these light codes.

To further understand the Grail light codes, they are subatomic particles of light in the DNA that are sparked within one's essence from the Great Creator. The purpose of the Grail codes is to ensure the ascension and evolutionary process for humanity to emerge into Christ and Unity Consciousness. As the daughter of Yeshua and Mary Magdalene, I carry the conjoined energies of their Divine Union within my DNA for I carry the cosmic intelligence of the Supreme Creator within my bloodline.

My parents' union represented the merging of the yin and the yang of the Divine Masculine and Divine Feminine energies in their purest forms. This is the spiritual meaning of alchemy of the merging of the marriage of the bride and bridegroom into Sacred Union as self-actualized beings. As their daughter, I hold the frequency of these conjoined energies as I embody the energy of Divine Oneness as the representation of the missing chalice at the Last Supper.

It is my sacred mission to continue my father's and mother's wisdom teachings, The Way. It is a path of integration and transformation that embraces both the Divine Masculine and Divine Feminine energies within the sacred heart of all souls. It is the inner path of Sacred Union taught by my parents. The wisdom teachings of The Way is the reclaiming of the divine Father-Mother-God essence of self-realization within all souls.

The ascension Grail codes activate the male-female aspect of one's spirit for their reunification to one's Divine Self. I, Sarah, wish to help awaken all souls to return to Divine Sacred Union as I continue to bring forth the wisdom teachings of The Way. Today, I ask you to open your hearts to unconditional love and holy grace so you may allow the Grail light codes to bring the integration of the male-female aspects to merge into Sacred Union with your I Am presence.

Dear ones, I take my role seriously as the Nurturer and Awakener, for I wish to bring peace, love, balance and harmony onto the planet for this is my sacred soul mission. Please allow me to help activate these new Grail codes within your being that are being infused upon this planet at this time. It is an extremely powerful time on the earth plane for these new light codes are awakening many souls at a very rapid rate.

At this time, the planet is undergoing a major purification process as the light codes are accelerating powerful earth changes. The earth changes are necessary to clear the lower vibrational frequencies of fear, anger, and chaos from the planet. At the time of the great fall of the civilization of Atlantis, fear became etched into the collective consciousness of humanity. As you merge into the Seventh Golden Age of Enlightenment, fear can no longer be held in the hearts of humanity or upon Mother Earth.

My mission is to help humanity raise their frequencies from fear into love so they may release the lower vibrational frequencies that have kept them entrapped upon the earth plane in fear. It is important that each soul takes responsibility for themselves and their own ascension process by releasing all lower vibrational frequencies held within their mental and emotional energetic bodies.

Releasing those frequencies will facilitate your return

to mental and emotional balance and assist my sacred mission to help all souls to return to Oneness during this new Golden Age of Enlightenment.

In the beginning when your divine spirit was sparked, your essence was created in Sacred Union and balance with All That Is. During many soul incarnations on this planet, humanity began to lose their connection to Oneness and fear and separation began to set in. The chaos and fear on this planet is a result of the separation of one's connection to the Supreme Creator. I, Sarah, come to open your hearts and help you to release your fear so you may return to the divine spark in which you were created.

It has been most unfortunate that many souls have lost their connection to God. The state of the world was meant to live in peace and joy, so I ask you to allow me to awaken your hearts and breathe in the energy of love and peace. As you breathe in this frequency, allow yourselves to listen to the still quiet voice from within.

What does your heart tell you? What does your intuition wish to share with you? Can you feel your soul returning to peace? I ask you, dear ones, to once again breathe in the energy of peace, love, harmony and balance as you let go of fear, hatred, and chaos that have kept you separate from God. Once again, breathe in the energy of love so you may live from your hearts and be at peace.

Allow me to open your hearts to my wisdom teachings as they are coded with powerful healing frequencies of love and light. My teachings will help you to live in the remembrance of the love that you are as you release fear from your hearts. Mother Earth is in need of your love. Mother Earth is in need of your peace. May you receive my wisdom teaching with an open heart so peace can prevail upon the planet.

It is an exciting time to see that more and more souls are awakening to God's love and light. The veils of forgetfulness are becoming thinner upon the planet as more souls are awakening to Spirit. Dear ones, this is how peace shall prevail; one soul at a time, one spark being reawakened.

I understand that there is a great deal of confusion regarding the ascension process, but it will soon pass as the planet is evolving into the fifth dimensional frequency. Perhaps this may sound counterintuitive, but the fear and chaos that is so prevalent within individuals is a sign that the purging of lower vibrational frequencies from the planet is working. You say, what does this mean? How can this be?

It means the collective consciousness of humanity's fear and separation is being purged at this time within all souls to be healed. The purification process can be quite painful, but it is necessary for the healing of humanity's base emotions to be released and transmuted into love. Be not afraid, dear ones, for this is a part of the Great Awakening, to help assist Mother Gaia and humanity to live in peace.

The Great Awakening of the ascension is indeed most powerful. As stated, there are many souls who are spiritually awakening at a very rapid rate. The mass ascension of many souls who are choosing to ascend through physical death must not frighten you for these souls are choosing to ascend on another dimensional level.

For those who choose to ascend rather than remain on the earth plane, it is necessary that they awaken to the higher vibrational frequencies of love, peace and joy during this powerful ascension period. As the earth is moving through this powerful shift in consciousness, may you allow yourselves to open your hearts for this will help to ease the pain and suffering that perhaps you may be feeling at this time.

I come as the Nurturer and Awakener to help humanity to receive the wisdom teachings of The Way, The Light and The Truth. May you receive this gift with an open heart and be the change you wish to see for Mother Earth is in need of you to return to love.

Go now, my children. Be at peace. Be at peace. Be at peace. And so it is.

Ascended Master Sarah

Chapter 4

Sarah,
the Nurturer and Awakener of Divine
Cosmic Love, Peace and Grace

Greetings, it is I, Sarah. I wish to share with you my sacred soul mission as the Nurturer and Awakener of Cosmic Divine Love, Peace and Holy Grace. I am here to empower you as a rite of passage into this new Golden Age of Enlightenment.

The only difference between my sacred soul mission and yours, is you do not need to be trained in the mystery schools to achieve enlightenment. I am here to awaken you to your own self-mastery. As a powerful lightworker, you have chosen to incarnate on Mother Gaia to anchor your love and light in order to bring peace to this planet.

During my lifetime, the energy upon the planet was very dense, dark, and heavy, and the majority of souls were spiritually unenlightened. Since the time of the Great Fall, when humanity separated from Oneness from the

Supreme Creator, it has been difficult for humanity to embody and embrace their true spiritual divinity. During this powerful ascension period, there is more light and love being admitted upon the planet which is awakening more souls to higher conscious teachings.

As I was born an advanced spiritual adept with my own inner gnosis, I was fortunate to be taught by my parents how to use my mystical powers as a goddess to transmute lower vibrational frequencies and emotions that are not of love.

My parents would often remind me that I was encoded with Divine Cosmic Love, Peace and Holy Grace as I was here to help others to show them The Way. As an advanced adept, I was able to cosmically align my energy into the earth and into the planetary crystalline grid to bring love, peace and balance onto the earth.

During my lifetime, Mother Earth held great density, fear and darkness and it was difficult to hold the vibration of the higher vibrational frequencies of love, peace, and balance onto the earth for any length of time. It is why Mother, Father and I worked diligently to imprint our energies of love and light into the earth for peace to prevail upon the planet.

It is my sacred soul mission to continue to reawaken humanity so that they, too, may be able to anchor their own energies of cosmic love, peace and grace upon the earth.

During this Great Awakening, the planet is undergoing great transformational changes. As the Nurturer and Awakener, I am infusing peace into the crystalline core of Mother Earth to help her during her ascension process. I am also infusing these frequencies within your own being to help you to remain balanced and stable as well.

At this time of the Great Awakening, may I invite you

to enter into the swing of worlds (into the higher realms of light) as you travel through time and space to re-remember your connection to God. Please take my hand as I lead you into the swing of worlds so that you may re-remember your connection to All That Is.

Please take a deep breath and allow me to help you to be at peace. When you are having difficulty mentally or emotionally or feeling unbalanced, I invite you to enter in to the swing between worlds and return to peace. It is my honor to assist you as you return to peace and merge into Divine Holy Sacred Union.

This is the balance of Divine Union that I speak of. I share my wisdom teachings with you today so that you may live in peace and in harmony with all of creation.

As a young girl, I idolized my parents for I knew they were special souls who were here to bring change to the world. I could feel their love and compassion for humanity as they had sacrificed themselves in order to complete their sacred soul mission. I was privileged to be their daughter and to continue the work that they had brought forth over 2,000 years ago.

The energy of love and peace that they had brought forward onto the earth at that time is now being reactivated once again. It is my honor to continue their mission to awaken all souls to the remembrance of who they truly are.

As the representation of the missing grail, I am here as their oracle, sharing their wisdom teachings so the planet and all of humanity may return to peace. This is a powerful time for more and more souls are awakening to the higher frequencies of cosmic love, peace and grace than any other time in history.

Today as I invoke these frequencies upon the earth, fear, anger and chaos shall begin to subside. The original energy of fear and separation from God can now be healed. This is the time of great celebration for all souls shall begin to awaken to the balanced energies of the Sacred Feminine and Sacred Masculine energies that my parents brought forth for all to receive.

As I bring this awareness to you, I ask you to embody your light so powerfully, so beautifully, so effervescently, that others will begin to feel and see the power of your light and love. As the planet is ascending into the fifth dimensional frequency, the veils of forgetfulness are becoming thinner and thinner, and more souls are awakening to their true spiritual essence.

Remember, dear ones, you are one such soul for you are making a difference as your light and your love is helping so many others to awaken as well.

I continue to reiterate this because it is most important that you merge with your I Am presence and be the change you wish to see upon your earth. Remember, dear ones, what my parents were able to do, you are able to do as well. Please allow yourselves to merge into divine sacred union with your I Am presence for this is the gift that my parents gave unto you.

My father was very courageous to accept his assignment of the great design to be crucified upon the cross. His devotion, his commitment unto humanity, was to show the world that the spirit lives on. My father continues to bring forth his powerful energy of love, peace and forgiveness for all to receive.

Dear ones, regardless of whether you understand the role that my mother and father played in the Great Design, it is cosmic love, peace and grace they wish for all to receive. May you allow your soul to be healed so that you may return to balance and be at peace.

Allow the troubles of the world to no longer affect you as you raise your vibrational frequencies into love and peace. Remember dear ones, live in the world but not of it. Just as Mother and Father were able to embody the frequencies of cosmic love, peace and grace into their own beings, I am here to help you to do the same.

Please allow me to help clear the density from your soul so that you may become a pure vessel of love and light, walking in divine balance upon Mother Gaia.

Please take my hand, and I will help you to return to Divine Sacred Union and be at peace. Know, dear ones, that there are many beings assisting the divine plan and bringing peace to this planet. There are multitudes of beings from other galactic and inner galactic star systems, planets, solar systems, and universes who are helping humanity and Mother Gaia to return to peace.

You, dear ones, are many of the star seeds who have chosen to assist Mother Gaia in her ascension process. You have forgotten your Oneness but are here once again to reawaken the remembrance of who you truly are to assist Mother Gaia during this powerful ascension process.

Dear ones, please accept this assignment as the beautiful star seed that you are to help awaken humanity to return to Oneness. It is my honor to bring the frequency of the Pearlescent White Flame of purity, love and innocence onto the planet at this time.

It was Mother Earth's original plan for every spirit to return to their original remembrance of their I Am presence. Mother Earth has sacrificed herself time and time again so that all souls could master their souls' journey to return to Oneness and to be at peace.

I ask you once again, dearest children, to breathe in the vibration of peace as you are all powerful messengers of love and light and you are bringing peace onto the planet. You are the living light of God's essence, and you are the change you wish to see.

Go now, my children. Be at peace. Bc at peace. Be at peace. And so it is.

Ascended Master Sarah

Chapter 5

Sarah,
Torchbearer of Divine Sacred Union

Greetings, it is I, Sarah. It is my honor and sacred soul mission to help every soul to return to balance and be at peace. Allow me to assist you in understanding how my mother and father brought forth sacred balance into their own lives and into my life as well.

When I was conceived, my parents' life force energy seeded the grail ascension light codes of Divine Union within my DNA. You, too, have the thread of Divine Holy Sacred Union within your own physical DNA. My parents were devoted to their sacred soul mission as they were deeply connected to the energy of All That Is.

During my parents' lives, they both struggled to be able to hold the divine balance within their own essences. At that time, the energy of earth held a great deal of fear, and it was very difficult for my mother and father to navigate through the dark and dense energy to be able to complete their souls' mission.

However, as advanced adepts and Ascended Masters, they were able to transmute the lower vibrational frequencies that were held within humanity's collective consciousness and infuse love and light into the earth. It was a difficult task, but they were able to bring healing onto the earth as they worked tirelessly to assist in transmuting the pain and suffering that had been etched into the earth.

To rejuvenate themselves during this most difficult time, they would often go into the Cave of Creation to seek respite. They entered into sacred ceremony and would ignite the ascension flame in order to spark their own I Am presence.

I was fortunate and blessed that when I became older, they allowed me to share in the sacred ceremony as well. We would sit in silence and use our breath to connect to the divine spark within us. Once we were able to connect to our own divine spark, we were able to unify our lower and higher selves and merge with our I Am presence.

This is how we rebalanced ourselves during the most difficult times of our lives. As we ignited the ascension flame and accessed the grail light codes into our being, we were able to merge into Divine Holy Sacred Union with our I Am presence.

I was grateful that my parents taught me these powerful sacred ceremonies as they were initiations into my own resurrection and ascension process. Mother always said that I was a quick study and she marveled how quickly I awakened to my own I Am presence. As I was born an awakened being the sacred ceremonies continued to spark within me remembrance of who I truly was on a deeper level.

Today I come to reawaken each of you to the divine remembrance of the truth of who you are. Many of you may feel the longing to seek Divine Union in your own lives. Please allow me to ignite the divine spark of God, of Holy Sacred Union, within you as I breathe into your heart chakra. As your divine spark awakens, may you re-remember your magnificence as a physical, spiritual being of light who has chosen to come to this earth plane at this time.

With your permission, may I activate your heart chakra, your throat chakra, your third eye, your crown chakra and your high heart to awaken to the divine light that you are? I am igniting the divine spark within you so that you may re-remember that you are a star seed who came to this planet to serve and to be served.

Each of you have chosen to come to this planet to help Mother Gaia during this powerful ascension process. It is of great importance that you remember that you are more than your physical body and that you are a powerful spirit who has come to assist in helping this planet return back to her original state of peace and love.

My mother, my father and I are here to remind you of your sacred mission and your sacred soul purpose. Please release any fear that you have that you are not able to complete your sacred mission. Dear ones, you are all magnificent beings of light who have chosen to sacrifice yourselves in order to assist this planet.

Dear ones, remember that you were all born with the love and the light of the Great Creator and I am here to ignite the divine spark within you here in the Cave of Creation.

I come as the Torchbearer of Light and Love to ignite

the flame of resurrection within you so that you may feel the resurrection of your own soul as you return to Divine Holy Sacred Union. Please remember that I am here infusing this most beautiful flame of resurrection inside of you where you may reawaken to the true essence of your being and to live in Divine Holy Sacred Union with all of creation.

Perhaps you are asking, what does it mean to live in Divine Holy Sacred Union? It simply means that you are living in harmony and balance with your true divine self, that you are living in harmony and balance with all of life. The eternal flame of Divine Holy Sacred Union was originally etched into your energy field at the inception of your spirit.

So breathe, dearest ones, breathe, into the eternal flame of resurrection to resurrect your soul so that you may return back to Divine Holy Sacred Union with All That Is.

Dear ones, there is a timeline for humanity to reawaken to sacred union and balance upon this planet, for the first 10,000-year cycle of peace on the planet has already begun. As Mother Earth ascends during this first 10,000-year cycle of peace, it is imperative that all souls reawaken to their original divine spirit.

Mother, Father and I will continue to assist in this Great Awakening until peace, love and balance are fully anchored into Mother Earth. Dear ones, as powerful spiritual beings, you have chosen to assist this planet to help her to return back to the original state of peace and love in which she was created. You are all brave spirits who have chosen to forget your Oneness to come in selfless service to assist Mother Gaia during this powerful ascension period.

Sacred Wisdom Teachings of Sarah

Do not become discouraged, dear ones, for we shall succeed, as I am passing the torch onto you so that you may reawaken more souls to re-remember their own sacred missions as well. As Sarah, Torchbearer of Divine Holy Sacred Union, I am passing the torch of peace, so that you may begin to embody the vibration of peace and love as it shall become etched onto the planet.

Remember, dearest children, you are powerful, powerful spirits who have come to bring change to the world, to bring peace to the world, to bring love to the world. Remember, dearest ones, you are the change you wish to see. It is my honor to pass the torch of peace onto you. Go now my children and be at peace.

Ascended Master Sarah

Lea Chapin

Chapter 6

Rebirthing
Into Oneness in the Cave of Creation

Greetings, it is I, Sarah. It is my honor to assist you to return to the path of integration, wholeness and oneness. I invite you to open your hearts to enter into the Cave of Creation. The Cave of Creation is the energy in which you were created for it is the original energy of the Father-Mother-God essence.

Today I invite you to enter into the Cave of Creation and allow yourself to feel the energy of peace, unity and love. Please allow me to help you to enter into the Cave of Creation as you breathe into your heart chakra so you may return to peace.

Please take a deep inhaling breath as you enter into the Cave of Creation, breathing in the essence of the healing energy of God's living light and love. Breathe into your heart, feeling the essence of the God and the Goddess that lives inside of you. It is here in the Cave of Creation that you are being rebirthed into your original state of Divine Holy Sacred Union. So breathe, my children, breathe. Breathe, my children, breathe.

In the course of our lifetime 2,000 years ago, my mother and father would go into the Cave of Creation when they needed to rejuvenate themselves during times of mental or emotional stress. I was also taught the sacred practice and I wish to share it with you today.

I know, dear ones, that it is difficult to reside on the earth plane where there is much fear, chaos and confusion. I invite you to enter into the Cave of Creation so that you may disconnect from the discordant energies that are causing you to be out of balance and live in fear.

So once again, take another deep breath, as you breathe in the vibration of peace. It is here in the Cave of Creation that you have the opportunity to release all that no longer serves you so that you may merge into the higher frequencies of cosmic love, peace and grace.

So breathe, my children, breathe. Breathe, my children, breathe, and allow yourselves to feel peace upon your souls. As you begin to breathe in these frequencies may you return to the balanced state of harmonious equanimity. Allow yourselves to be filled with the loving light of God as you become a vessel of pure love and light.

During the age of Pisces, there was great duality in human consciousness due to fear, chaos, conflict and violence. Those days were filled with great angst as the patriarchal rule created division in the hearts of mankind. It was the common belief that God lived outside of oneself, and many lived in fear and confusion about their connection to God.

In this new era of the Golden Age of Enlightenment, there is a grand opportunity for a mass awakening of the

Christ Consciousness in all souls. Since the Great Fall when mankind had been veiled from their inner gnosis, it has been difficult for humanity to feel the power of their divine selves. It is why I invite you to enter into the Cave of Creation so that you may return to Oneness and feel the true essence of your own divine souls.

Once again, dear ones, I ask you to breathe. Breathe in the energy of the white light of God, filling your heart with peace, love, compassion and mercy. Today you are being rebirthed as a new earth being for this is a grand opportunity to transmute fear into love.

As you begin to breathe in the power of God's living light, you shall merge with your higher self and return to the original state of your divine Essent self. I ask you, dear ones, can you imagine if every soul on this planet was at peace, how would the world change if people honored the divine Father-Mother-God essence within themselves?

How would the world be changed if the Sacred Feminine was honored? If mankind valued intuition, creativity, compassion, kindness, and love instead of valuing money, power, control, greed, how would the world change if everyone lived in Oneness and honored and respected all of life?

How would the world change if humanity began to listen to the voice of Great Spirit and honored Mother Gaia and all of creation? Can you imagine the world returning back to a place of peace and balance? There would be no more hatred, fear, war, or anger. Imagine a world fill with peace where all lived in harmony and balance as they were originally intended and created to be. Can you imagine all souls honoring themselves and respecting all of life?

Dear ones, this was the reality during the heightened civilizations of Lemuria and Atlantis where all lived in balance with all of creation and it is possible for this to occur again. This is why I am bringing this to your attention because many of you have lived in those heightened civilizations and had once lived in balance and in harmony with all of life.

Perhaps this is why you are feeling the longing to return to balance and to be at peace, because your cellular memory has been reawakened with the remembrance of how you once lived. You have had many lifetimes, living in balance as a physical spiritual being on earth. Indeed, it is possible for you to live this way once again.

Dear ones, allow yourselves to enter into the Cave of Creation so that you may be at peace. There is no need to fear for all is in divine order. Can you trust yourselves to surrender to the unified force field in the Cave of Creation?

Can you feel the merging of Sacred Union within yourselves? Are you able to feel peace and tranquility from the depths of your souls? We know, dear ones, it is not easy, but it can be done.

I, Sarah, have chosen to help assist humanity to reawaken to its remembrance for I had achieved Sacred Union during my own lifetime as the daughter of Yeshua and Mary Magdalene. I am not saying I did not have my struggles, but I knew how to unify and rebalance myself rather quickly when I was out of balance.

I was blessed to have the knowledge and the training that I bring to you at such an early age. So once again, breathe in the energy of the white light of God as you breathe in the energy of peace, tranquility, energy and love, as you allow yourselves to rest in the Cave of Creation.

Dear ones, as you embody the energy of peace, it will

become contagious, just like the hundred-monkey syndrome, your peace will affect many more souls. As more and more souls begin to spiritually awaken, this is how peace and love shall prevail upon the planet, one soul at a time.

The earth is in need of your love as she is absorbing the pain and the suffering of humankind. The pain and suffering that has been emitted upon the earth has caused Mother Earth great pain and sorrow. It is imperative that three-fourths of humanity spiritually awaken in order for Mother Earth to be at peace.

Dear ones, I ask you to take another deep breath and begin to breathe in the essence of peace as you feel the reunification of your own soul here in the Cave of Creation. Breathe, my children, breathe. Breathe, my children, breathe. Breathe, my children, breathe. Open yourselves up to this beautiful frequency of peace as you surrender, trust, allow and receive, the energy of peace upon your souls.

Once again, I ask you to breathe in the power of peace as you merge with your higher self and merge in Sacred Union with your I Am presence. May you accept this gift that I bring unto you this day as you become aware of a warm golden light emitting from your heart. Breathe into your high heart and expand the light to fill your entire body with love.

Perhaps you are hearing the sound of Om emitting from your heart; this is the sound and the energy of the God essence. Om is the sound of the invisible unified force field of divine love as spoken by the great I Am. Feel the power and the love as you receive this powerful frequency.

I invite you to merge your higher self and your oversoul with your I Am presence so that you may return to Divine Holy Sacred Union. May you return to love as you awaken to your full self-mastery.

Dear ones, I thank you for allowing me to assist you here in the Cave of Creation so that you may return to a state of peace, harmony, and grace. May you live in joy and remembrance of who you truly are. Go in peace. Go in peace. Go in peace.

Ascended Master Sarah

Chapter 7

Reconnecting with Mother Gaia to Return to Love

Greetings, it is I, Sarah. Mother Gaia, our earth mother, wishes to bring love and peace from the very crystalline core of her heart into the hearts of all sentient beings. My own mother, Mary, taught me that Mother Gaia was our earth mother, and we should honor her and respect her as we were to honor and respect ourselves.

My mother spoke of Mother Gaia's sacrifice and how she had allowed herself to be inhabited by humans in order for humanity to forget their Oneness. As part of the Great Design, it was designed for all souls to forget their personal Oneness with the Supreme Creator, which created the current imbalance of fear, chaos, war and violence that is rampant on your planet at this time.

It has been most unfortunate that this has occurred, but Mother Earth has allowed it and has sacrificed herself for the human soul journey.

In your current civilization, the Great Awakening has begun as more souls are awakening to their higher consciousness. More and more souls are awakening to the living light and love of God's essence as they realign themselves to the universal consciousness of All That Is.

Mother Earth is undergoing her ascension process into the fifth dimensional frequency and there is a timetable for her to return back to her original state as the planet of love. The purification process of the ascension is creating great chaos and dissention upon the planet.

The massive earth changes that are occurring are necessary for Mother Earth to ascend and to clear the lower vibrational frequencies that mankind has emitted upon the earth. Until three-fourths of humanity spiritually awakens, the purification process of the earth will continue.

It is unfortunate that your current civilization lives in glass houses and are disconnected from the earth. Humans were designed to live in harmony with the Earth Mother and all of Great Spirit. Unfortunately, mankind has disconnected energetically from the earth which has caused confusion and despair in the human psyche.

Many humans have lost their own innate connection to the Earth Mother and to all of creation and are unable to tap into their own innate wisdom. That is why so many are mentally, emotionally and physical out of balance, as they are disconnected from the heart of Mother Gaia.

I ask you to take time each day to connect to the Earth Mother and feel her loving presence, even if it is for a moment. Perhaps you may wish to hug a tree or admire a beautiful flower or simply begin to inhale the energy of the earth, feeling her sweet nectar. Please allow yourselves to connect to the energy of the earth, for it will help you to find your way. It will help you to return to balance and to be at peace.

As the Sacred Feminine and Sacred Masculine energies are reawakening upon the planet, it is important to stay grounded upon the earth as these new energies are indeed most powerful. If one is not grounded, these powerful frequencies can create an imbalance in those who are mentally or emotionally unstable.

It is why you are seeing such erratic behaviors in the human population because these powerful frequencies are affecting the human psyche at a very deep and profound level. These frequencies can be most disturbing to one's soul if they are unable to stay connected to the energy of Mother Gaia.

It is imperative that during these transformational times that every soul begin to listen to the still quiet voice from within in order to stay balanced, centered and to be at peace. By staying centered and listening to your own inner voice, you will be able to navigate your own emotions during these most challenging times. It is unfortunate that so many souls have lost connection to their own innate wisdom.

As you connect to the energy of Mother Earth, may you feel her love for you as she helps you to reconnect to your own soul. I remind you that you are able to go into the Cave of Creation to heal your own pain and suffering and to return to balance.

I ask you to place your feet upon the ground and connect to the energy of Mother Earth and breathe in the energy of peace in the Cave of Creation. Allow yourselves to release all that no longer serves you so that you may return to peace and re-remember your true divinity.

In the next several years, there will be many advanced

souls who will incarnate on the planet who are great avatars, bringing peace, love, and light onto the planet. They will be bringing a powerful vibrational frequency onto the planet that will assist humanity to ascend and spiritually awaken at a very rapid rate.

Perhaps you are already feeling this energy as I speak. These magnificent souls are choosing to incarnate at this time for the planet is in dire straits and there is an urgency for humanity and all of life to return to balance and to be at peace.

As humanity returns to balance and lives in harmony with Mother Gaia, there will be no need for the chaotic weather patterns or the earth changes. Mother Earth will no longer have a need to purify herself of lower discordant energies.

Dear ones, I remind you if you are living in harmony with the Earth Mother, you will always be protected and safe. When you stay grounded and connected unto her and listen to your own innate wisdom, you will be able to know where to go, what to do, in times of danger, just like the migratory animals and birds who rely on their instinct to be safe.

Dear ones, allow yourselves to connect to the energy in the crystalline core of Mother Earth as you allow her to clear any and all mental or emotional distortions in your energy field that are causing you to be out of balance. Humankind has been out of balance due to all that is not of nature: cement buildings, skyscrapers, artificial grass, GMOs, and all that is not the original creation of Great Spirit.

Today, I place a protective shield around you with the Silver Ray of light. It is my gift to you to protect you from the disharmonic frequencies that are being emitted upon the planet at this time. Please use the Silver Ray to protect yourselves energetically from the lower vibrational frequencies that are affecting this planet. I wish to bring this to you today for it is my sacred mission to help all souls return to balance and to be at peace.

My mother gifted me with the knowledge of the Silver Ray when I was a very young girl. I used it during stressful times when I felt disconnected from myself. It is a powerful frequency that will assist you to reconnect to your innate wisdom. I used this special ray when I was in the land of Avalon during the early years of my life.

The energy in England, Ireland and Scotland was some of the most powerful frequencies that I had ever felt during my lifetime. As I connected to the heart of Mother Earth in Avalon, I used the Silver Ray to rebalance myself into the essence of the land. The land felt so magical and healing unto my soul.

To this day, the energy of the region of Glastonbury and Avalon remains a powerful energy vortex. The land continues to be magical and healing. It is why so many are drawn there and recognize my essence there in the land. It is also enhanced as the special energy of the Druids and the Celtic Gods and Goddesses once lived in that holy sacred land.

The land is truly balanced and is a powerful vortex for healing to occur. If you feel emotionally or mentally unstable, call into the magic of Avalon and it will bring healing and balance to your soul.

Dear ones, I ask you, do not be afraid that you are not able to manage this for you are all living masters and if you so choose, please listen to the still quiet voice from within and connect to the energy of Mother Gaia and into the energy of Avalon.

The Great Awakening has now begun, and it is imperative as a new earth being that you connect yourself to the energy of Mother Gaia during this powerful ascension process that is occurring on the planet at this time. I ask you once again to honor yourself, love yourself and listen to the still, quiet voice within, listen from your heart as you feel the love of Mother Gaia as she helps you to return to love and to be at peace.

Go now, my children. Be at peace. Be at peace. Be at peace. And so it is.

Ascended Master Sarah

Chapter 8

The Power of Divine Sophia to Heal the Wounds of the Sacred Feminine

Greetings, it is I, Sarah. It is time for the Divine Feminine to rise again in her full power. Throughout the course of history, the power of the Divine Feminine has been suppressed. This has created a great imbalance in the world as the Sacred Feminine energy has been stifled for fear of her power.

In your current civilization, this suppression has created an imbalance upon the earth. The unbalanced masculine energy of the old patriarchal rule of control, greed, power and rule, has become a predominant force affecting the imbalance upon the earth.

As the voice of the Sacred Feminine rises again, she will come back into her full power. Can you imagine if humanity valued the sacred mother, and all lived in harmony and balance with all of creation?

Dear ones, the power of Divine Sophia has returned to heal the planet. Today, I, Sarah, wish to bring healing to each of you so that you may heal the wounds of the suppressed feminine energies that have affected you. It does not matter if you are male or female, as the suppression of the Sacred Feminine has affected all souls upon the planet.

Wars have been fought due to the fear of the power of the Sacred Mother. The misguided and imbalanced male energies that have created chaos upon the planet can now be healed by the return of the Sacred Feminine. It is my desire to bring a healing to all those who have suffered from the suppression of the Sacred Feminine throughout the course of time.

It is imperative that the unbalanced male and female aspects of your one's soul be healed. Divine Mother Sophia is here to help heal the wounds of the past so that humanity may live in peace and balance once again.

Today, I, Sarah, empower you with Divine Sophia's essence as you feel her power inside of your being. I wish to help heal the abuse and the trauma that was caused by the old patriarchal rule throughout the course of history. It pleases me to see the rise of the Sacred Feminine standing in her full power once again.

An example is the #metoo movement in your current civilization. This movement has ignited the voice of the feminine to rise again as she returns back to her rightful position upon the earth. That combination of voices created powerful change. The voice of the Sacred Feminine is a powerful force, a gift to every soul who is in need of healing.

I invoke the power of the Divine Mother Sophia to bring healing to all souls on the planet. Her energy is a very real, palpable energy. I ask you to feel her energy in your heart so you may heal the wounds of the past that no longer serve you.

If you so shall, breathe in the energy of Divine Mother Sophia as she helps you to heal your soul. It is my honor to assist you to access the Sacred Feminine essence through the power of your breath. So breathe, my children, breathe. Breathe, my children, breathe.

My mother was a High Priestess of Goddess Isis, and she taught my own mother how to access the energy of Divine Mother through her breath. My mother would use this technique when she was afraid or felt disconnected from her own divine power.

Mother taught me how to call forth the energy of Divine Mother Sophia during times of stress. Our lives were often in peril, and it helped me to rebalance myself and to feel my inner strength and power once again. My mother was a very strong woman, but she often struggled just as you to embody the power of Divine Sophia during times of stress.

I ask you to take a deep breath and breathe in the energy of Divine Mother Sophia so you may feel her strength and power upon your soul. Dear ones, feel the energy of Divine Mother Sophia as a powerful force field surrounding your energy field with love, healing, strength and compassion.

I wish to share with you that I, Sarah, embody the strength of the Divine Feminine but I also embody the strength of the Divine Masculine. As I was created in sacred union, I am here to help you embody the balanced male-female aspects of yourselves so that you may begin to heal from the wounds of the past.

Please take a deep breath and call in the frequency of

the balanced Divine Masculine energy as you allow it to merge with your Divine Feminine essence. Now I wish for you to take another deep breath and feel your Divine Feminine essence supporting the unbalanced masculine aspect of yourselves that has been wounded.

By embracing both the yin and the yang aspects of your spiritual nature, you shall achieve Divine Holy Sacred Union. This is the energy of completion that you are all seeking: wholeness, balance and integration of your own soul. This is the spiritual union that is needed for healing Mother Gaia and all of humanity.

The power of the Sacred Feminine is the secret to healing yourself and bringing peace and healing unto the world. May you allow me to activate each of you as portals of peace. As peacekeepers and way showers of love and light you shall heal the world.

As you receive this activation, you will become a lighthouse for peace and love. May you receive this with an open heart as the world needs peace and love.

Divine Mother Sophia has stepped forward to bring peace, love, compassion, and balance on the earth for the misguided masculine has ruled the planet for too long. I ask you to honor yourselves as you are now living portals of peace, love and light.

Today I invoke Archangel Michael, calling in his Blue Ray of light. I ask you to breathe in the Blue Ray of light and feel his strength as he helps you to feel the power of your divine sacred self. Archangel Michael will continue to help you to heal the wounds of the past so that you may be at peace.

This is a powerful time, dear ones, as the return of the Divine Feminine merges into her full power. It is my honor to bring Divine Sophia's love onto the planet for all to receive. The power of Divine Mother Sophia will heal the wounds of the unbalanced male and female aspects in all souls and then, and only then, will the planet return back to its original state of balance and peace in which it was created.

Go now, my children. Be at peace. Be at peace. Be at peace. And so it is.

Ascended Master Sarah

Chapter 9

Releasing
the Old Patriarchal Rule
of Fear and Separation

Greetings, it is I, Sarah. It is my honor to share the return of the Divine Feminine as she is healing the old patriarchal rule of fear and control that has created havoc and despair upon the earth plane. It is an exciting time for the Sacred Feminine has reemerged, as her energy can no longer be suppressed or denied.

It is my mission to help heal the old patriarchal rule that has controlled and ruled this planet for far too long. The voice of Divine Sophia has returned in her full power for the healing that is so needed for this planet.

Dearest children, allow the energy of the Sacred Feminine to heal the unbalanced masculine energy of control, fear and chaos that has affected humanity and the world at large. Planet Earth is undergoing a powerful transformational process as she ascends into the fifth dimension.

This powerful transformation and purification process has been quite difficult as it appears as if the world is coming to an end. Indeed, the world is coming to an end as you know it, for the old patriarchal rule is slowly falling away.

Dear ones, this is a grand opportunity to align yourselves with Divine Mother Love. She is here to help you to heal the lower vibrational frequencies of fear, control, chaos, and separation that have kept you disconnected from your true spiritual essence.

During the age of Pisces, the astrological symbol of the two complementary fish symbolized the reciprocal balance between the male and female aspects in a balanced partnership. During this age, the Divine Masculine and Feminine aspects were meant to create Sacred Union that was needed in order to be awakened to the Christ Consciousness.

However, this did not occur as the unbalanced masculine energy was unable to honor the sacred feminine energy. This inability has created the world to be out of balance and in a state of chaos.

I, Sarah, have come to help humanity embody the energy of the Divine Mother so that the unbalanced masculine energies can no longer control or suppress Divine Mother's power. It is now time that the Divine Mother can return back to her rightful place upon this planet.

Dear ones, can you imagine the world to be rebirthed as a planet of peace, love, harmony and balance once again? Many of you once lived in sacred union with all of life during the heightened civilizations of Lemuria and Atlantis.

It is why so many of you are seeking and searching for the missing grail as you are seeking balance and sacred union within your own lives. As you embody the sacred feminine into your being, you shall be the change you wish to see in the world. By merging with the energy of Divine Mother, you shall return to peace.

The planet is in need of peace, and you are all masters who have the capacity to create with the power of your thoughts. Quantum physics reveals that the entire universe is alive with consciousness and all life is connected. One's thoughts and feelings affect reality at a subatomic level.

This means that what you believe and project out into the world can actually affect one's life. The more fear, hate and anger you program into your thinking, the more you create that reality. The more kindness, love and compassion you project onto the world, the more you create love and peace on planet earth.

Can you imagine a world filled with peace where all live in harmony and balance? John Lennon's song, "Imagine" was just that. He wrote the beautiful lyrics, "May you say I am a dreamer, but I am not the only one. I dream someday you will join me, and the world will be one."

This is not something new, dearest ones. You have all done this before. You are just being reminded. Can you feel peace? Can you sense peace? Are you ready to live in a world filled with peace? Dearest children, this is indeed possible as it begins with one soul at a time. You are just re-remembering how to create it again.

When I was a young child, Mother taught me how to access Divine Sophia's ancient wisdom teachings and she would often lead me in meditation as we astral traveled to the etheric mystery schools of Egypt. Mother was an initiate of Priestess Isis, the Goddess of Wisdom, and she was able to access the wisdom in the sacred etheric temples as we would re-remember our divine purpose.

We would sit for hours meditating in the temples as our pineal glands would become activated with full remembrance of the power of divine mother love. Many of you also lived in Egypt and were initiates of Priestess Isis. I have come today to reawaken these memories of Divine Sophia's ancient wisdom within your beings.

Mother and I wish to invite you into the etheric temple of oneness and remembrance so that you shall reawaken to your sacred divine feminine power. As you awaken to the remembrance of Divine Sophia may you feel the expansion of your heart chakra merging with the energy of Divine Mother Love.

As your pineal gland begins to reawaken to the ancient wisdom teachings that are your birthright, as you allow your mind, body, and spirit to return to love. This will shift and clear the lower vibrational frequencies of fear, control and separation from your being.

I ask you to take in a deep inhaling breath and allow Divine Mother to assist you in opening your heart so that you may be at peace. As you reawaken to the wisdom teachings of Divine Mother, you will no longer be controlled by the old patriarchal rule of fear, control and chaos.

As you deepen your connection to your Divine Mother Love, imagine the potential and possibilities that can happen when all of life returns to peace. Today as we assist you here in the etheric temples, may you return to love and be at peace. Breathe in the power of Divine Mother as she is here to help you to reawaken to your full divine power.

You are all divine sovereign beings, and it is time that you merged in Divine Sacred Union with your I Am presence. May you receive this gift with an open heart as you "join me and the world will be as one."

Go now, my children, and prepare yourselves to receive, to open your hearts to Divine Mother Love. Go in peace. Go in peace. Go in peace. And so it is.

Ascended Master Sarah

Chapter 10

Opening
Your Heart Chakra
to Divine Mother Love

Greetings, it is I, Sarah. I invite you to open your heart to the power of Divine Mother Love. May you feel her love as I open your heart chakra to the energy of Divine Mother. I invite you to breathe in the power of the living light of God feeling the essence and the presence of Divine Mother within your own soul.

This is a powerful time on earth as the energy of the sacred feminine has reemerged upon the planet. Today as I invoke the essence of the sacred feminine, allow your heart chakra to open to the beautiful essence of divine mother love. May you feel your heart chakra radiating and feeling the essence of God's living light upon your soul.

When I was a young child, my mother taught me how to tap into the power of the sacred feminine energy. She taught me how to use my breath to connect through my heart into the heart of the Divine Mother. When I would breathe into my high heart I would often feel an intense vibration as if I was levitating out of my body into an altered state of consciousness.

During those moments, I could feel the expansion of my high heart opening within me and encompassing me with divine mother love. I was extremely sensitive, and as an empath, I could feel her love as it penetrated into every cell, fiber and pore of my being. I felt tremendous love, peace and bliss as my consciousness merged with my I Am presence.

As a young child, I was able to tap into this practice without much difficulty for I was fairly proficient, though mother had to watch me carefully for I could have easily left my body if not properly grounded. This practice and its purpose was designed to help me merge with my higher self and merge in sacred union with my I Am presence.

My human awareness no longer existed, and I felt divine communion with parts of myself that I had forgotten had existed in my conscious awareness. I would often feel the loving presence of Divine Sophia encompassing me and it felt like pure bliss and pure ecstasy upon my own soul.

I invite you to journey with me as I lead you in meditation to commune with your own I Am presence. I ask you to breathe into your own high heart and allow Divine Mother to awaken you so you may return to Divine Holy Sacred union within yourselves. Breathe into your high heart and allow Divine Mother's energy to bathe you in her loving presence. May you open your heart to unconditional love and may the essence of peace be upon your soul.

As the daughter of Yeshua and Mary Magdalene I was

privileged to be taught the power of the sacred feminine. Even though I was born an awakened spirit, my mother taught me to reconnect to my own divine power. She helped me to strengthen my auric field so that I could connect to my higher self as she showed me how to open up my high heart to connect to my own Divine Sophia wisdom.

Today, I invite you to breathe into your heart chakra so that you may reconnect to your own ancient wisdom. May you breathe into this energy as you feel the essence of your soul connecting with divine mother love. Allow your spirit, your mind and your body to be bathed in the healing energy of divine mother love. Accept this gift as it truly is your connection to All That Is.

I know, dearest ones, that the soul's journey has not been easy for many of you. Many of you have lived numerous lifetimes that have been most challenging and difficult. I see that you are in need of rest and healing for it is no wonder, dearest ones, that you feel disconnected from your true Essent self.

The challenges of living on the earth can be quite demanding and challenging, but please allow me to help you to reconnect to your I Am presence. Once again, take a deep breath, connect with the energy of divine mother love. Know that this powerful frequency of the divine feminine energy will heal all that ails you and allow you to return to balance and to be at peace.

Dear ones, can you feel the energy drifting within your consciousness, within your physicality and within your own soul? Can you feel peace encompassing your heart chakra? Perhaps you are feeling lighter and lighter as I speak as I am assisting you to merge with your higher self and with your I Am presence. Allow the energy of divine mother love to help heal you from the wounds of the past that no longer serve you.

I, Sarah, come forth as the representation of the Black Madonna for it is the energy of the hidden aspects of the Divine Mother that I hold and carry. The divine feminine has been hidden and veiled throughout time due to the suppression of the patriarchal rule.

It is time for Divine Mother to step forward and allow her voice to be heard as the sacred feminine is no longer to be suppressed. As the representation of the Black Madonna, I come to bring the energy of divine feminine to the planet in her most powerful and potent form. Her energy is both strong and yet is gentle.

Allow me to bring the energy of the Divine Mother into the chamber of your high heart so that you may be empowered in your own Sacred Feminine energy. I am bringing the energy of the Divine Mother to you as a gift as your power, your light, your love, is so needed to bring peace to planet earth. As lightworkers, you are assisting this planet to return to peace.

Therefore, it is necessary that you embody the energy of Divine Mother in order to heal the old patriarchal rule. As lightworkers, you all hold and carry the secrets of the divine feminine. The power of the Great Mother is intricately woven into the hidden wisdom that you each hold and carry as your birthright.

My mother, Mary Magdalene, wishes to step forward to help strengthen your connection to Divine Sophia. Just as she helped me to strengthen my connection, she is stepping forward to help you strengthen your connection as well. My mother embodies the sacred feminine essence in a balanced, unified force field within her own essence.

She comes today to help you to unify and strengthen

your own force field of energy so that you may step into your own divine power. Mother and I are bringing this energy unto you, for this is a part of your own ascension process as you merge with your I Am presence and achieve self-mastery.

Dear ones, breathe in the energy of Divine Mother Love as my mother, Mary, opens your high heart so that you may feel the unconditional love within your own being. Mother and I come to bring you this gift to anchor the energy of Divine Mother within your own essence so that you may share her with the world. Dear ones, feel the essence of Divine Holy Sacred Union within your own soul as you return to peace.

Today, we call forth the balance of the Sacred Feminine energy so it may open your high heart to merge with your Sacred Masculine energy. This initiation into Divine Holy Sacred Union is an initiation into the chamber of the sacred heart.

It allows you to achieve self-realization and merge with your I Am presence. Please allow your spirit to receive this initiation as a remembrance of who you truly are as a divine child of God.

As I give thanks to my own mother for helping me to re-remember and to empower me in the process of opening my own high heart, I wish to gift you with this as well. May you receive this with the love in which it was given. Go now, my children. Prepare yourselves to receive as you open your high heart to divine mother love and to merge in divine holy sacred union with your I Am presence.

Go now, my children. Be at peace. Be at peace. Be at peace. And so it is.

Ascended Master Sarah

Chapter 11

Stepping Into Your Still Point to Remember Your Divine Self

Greetings, dear ones, it is I, Sarah. I come to teach you how to connect your breath to your still point. The still point is the path of inner connection to God, which is called "gnosis." It is in the silence of not doing where you are able to listen.

"Listening to your own heart, finding out who you are, is not simple. It takes time for the chatter to quiet down. In the silence of not doing, you are able to know what you feel, if you listen from your heart, what is being offered is that anything can be your guide. Listen."

Dear ones, your still point is located within your high heart. As you breathe into your high heart, may you feel the silence of your own soul. Perhaps, dearest children, this technique may seem foreign to you, but you have all done it through many lifetimes before.

I am here to help you to reconnect and listen to your own soul. So breathe, my children, breathe. Breathe into your high heart chakra, breathing into the still point. As you breathe into your still point, may you begin to feel the power of your own divine spirit.

Are you able to listen to the still quiet voice of your own innate wisdom? Can you feel the presence of the living God inside of you?

I ask you once again to take another deep breath, breathe into your high heart as you breathe into your still point. It is here within the still point that you are able to feel God's love and light and be at peace. As you awaken to your own inner guidance, begin to invoke the words, "I Am."

By invoking the words, "I Am," you are invoking the divine spark of the God/Goddess within you. Use this practice to calm yourselves, rebalance yourselves during times of stress. As you access the energy of the Great I Am, the heart chakra shall expand, and you will begin to feel a sense of peace and calmness.

As you invoke the words, "I Am," this is the divine spark of your I Am presence to which you have been longing to connect in Divine Holy Sacred Union.

I AM THAT I AM! I AM THAT I AM! I AM THAT I AM!

This is the practice that my mother taught me from the mystery schools in Egypt and that I have come to share with you today. As Mother would lead me into meditation, we would invoke the power of the Great I Am as we were able to listen to our own inner truth.

During these sacred ceremonies, Mother and I were able to feel the essence of our own oversouls merging into Oneness. Dear ones, I ask you to use this technique to breathe into your still point during times of stress. Understand, dear ones, that the soul's journey can be most challenging, but please use this technique so that you may return to balance and to be at peace. It is important that you have access to this technique to use when life and all its struggles become confusing. It is necessary to use discernment and listen to your own inner guidance during times of confusion. As you listen to the still quiet voice within, this is the road map to achieving self-mastery. Once again, I ask you to take a deep breath and breathe into your still point.

I AM THAT I AM! I AM THAT I AM! I AM THAT I AM!

Can you feel the energy rising with you as you merge your higher self with your I Am presence? This is the key to merging into Divine Holy Sacred Union with All That Is. This is the key to return to balance and to be at peace.

I AM THAT I AM! I AM THAT I AM! I AM THAT I AM!

Mother Earth is undergoing a major transformational shift into this new Golden Age of Enlightenment and it is by accessing the still point that you, too, shall be able to ascend in consciousness with her as well. You have chosen to be here on this planet at this time as a powerful lightworker bringing hope, peace and inspiration unto the world. You are here to make a difference as you are the change you wish to see. Can you feel your high heart expanding as you breathe into your still point, as you bring your love and your light unto the world? You are a powerful physical, spiritual being of God's living light and love. So once again, I ask you to breathe into the still point as you feel the power of the love that you are. As you embody the power of love and peace within your essence, may you live in joy and remembrance of who you truly are.

As you breathe into your still point and release the lower vibrational frequencies of worry, fear, and anxiety, you will begin to feel the vibration of joy. Joy is the totality of All That Is for it is the energy of the God essence. When you embody the vibration of joy, you have come home to yourself. So, once again, please invoke, "I AM THAT I AM! I AM THAT I AM! I AM THAT I AM!"

Dear ones, allow your heart to open as you feel the power of God as you breathe into your still point and return to peace. Go now, my children. Be at peace. Be at peace. Be at peace. And so it is.

Ascended Master Sarah

Lea Chapin

Chapter 12

Infusing
the New Grail Light Codes
Onto the Planet

Greetings, my beloveds, it is I, Sarah. It is with great excitement that I wish to share with you the new Holy Grail light codes that are being emitted upon the planet at this time. These new light codes are imprinting and infusing love, harmony, balance, and peace upon the planet. As the daughter of Yeshua and Mary Magdalene, I am honored to be the guardian of these new Holy Grail light codes as I carry the frequency of their energy within my essence.

Dear ones, please take a deep breath and allow me to infuse the new light codes within your beings. Dear ones, as you embody the essence of these powerful frequencies, understand that they are healing the lower vibrational frequencies that have been held within your souls.

I do not wish to frighten you, but these light codes hold

tremendous power and are quite potent. If you are not centered and grounded, you may not be able to embody these frequencies in their fullest essence. Once again, I ask you to ground yourselves to Mother Earth so that you may stay centered and balanced. So breathe, my children, breathe. Breathe in these powerful light codes.

These codes are lightly infusing peace upon the planet like soft summer raindrops. Many individuals are capturing these frequencies through the lenses of their cameras as they are able to see the beautiful spectrum of the rainbow colors that are emerging upon the planet.

Dear ones, I tell you that more and more peace is being imprinted upon the earth than you can imagine. There are many celestial beings of light from other galaxies, universes, solar systems, and planets that are helping to bring these powerful light codes onto the planet.

Can you sense a change in the air? Can you feel peace that is now emerging upon the planet? Perhaps you say, "No, I cannot, for there is too much chaos, anger, violence and war upon the planet. How can peace truly prevail?"

Dear ones, please know that there is a timetable for the planet to return back to her original state as the planet of love and peace. You are in the Great Awakening of the first 10,000 year cycle of peace. It is a powerful transformational period that is often compared to a birthing process.

Understand that it may seem difficult, but it is necessary as the Holy Grail codes are bringing healing to the planet during this powerful transformational period. Dear ones, you, also, may be going through your own dark night of the soul and your own transformational period. I ask you to open your heart to receive the new Holy Grail light codes that will help you soften and heal during your own ascension.

During my lifetime, Mother, Father and I would often go into the Cave of Creation, and we would call in the Holy Light Grail codes to rejuvenate our minds, bodies and spirits. We would sit for hours meditating and invoking the light codes into our consciousness to deepen our connection to our I Am presence.

During these sacred activations, we often felt a powerful connection to our own spirit as we connected through our own pineal gland. We knew that by etching our energies into our own essence, it would help awaken the frequencies of cosmic love, peace and grace upon the earth.

Today, I come to help awaken you to the Holy Grail light codes as you awaken your own pineal gland so you may connect to your own I Am presence. As you receive these light codes, know that you are being upgraded energetically to be able to hold more love, light and peace within your physical and etheric bodies.

The light codes are coming in more powerfully because the energy of the planet is able to receive them, thus allowing the light codes to be accessed by humankind. Dear ones, please by mindful how you access and use the light codes for they are indeed most powerful.

So breathe, my children, breathe. Allow me to help you to access the light codes so that you will return to balance and be at peace. Please breathe into your still point so that you may access these codes in a safe and balanced manner.

Dear ones, when your spirit essence split into the two aspects of your sacred masculine and sacred feminine essence, the search to reunify with your higher self became an unconscious desire. It is by invoking the Holy Grail light codes that you are able to reunify and return to Oneness in Sacred Union with the Divine Masculine/Divine Feminine aspects of your spirit.

So breathe, my children, breathe. Breathe in the new light codes as you return to Divine Holy Sacred Union with your spirit.

In your current civilization, many are searching for the other half of themselves and are seeking to find their better half. Dear ones, understand that what you are seeking is your own divine sacred spark. What you are seeking is the reunification of your spirit with your own I Am presence.

The truth is, you are looking to unify and partner with your own divine spark. This is the divine union that some are most desperately seeking. Remember, the search no longer continues for the search is inside of yourselves.

Dearest children, breathe in the Holy Grail light codes and allow the reunification of the divine spirit to merge in Sacred Union with your I Am presence. Today, I come to help you embody these codes within your essence. May you allow me to assist you? May I touch your crown chakra as I activate your crown chakra to seed the new Holy Grail light codes within your being?

May I touch your third eye to activate and allow yourselves to see the new Holy Grail light codes within your being? May I touch your throat chakra so that you may receive these new Holy Grail light codes within your being?

May I touch your heart chakra so that you may receive these new Holy Grail light codes within your being? May I touch your high heart so that you may receive these new Holy Grail codes within your being?

May I touch your sacral chakra to receive these new

Holy Grail light codes within your being? May I touch your root chakra so that you may receive these new Holy Grail light codes within your being? May I activate your earth star chakra through the soles of your feet to anchor the Holy Grail light codes within the crystalline core of Mother Earth?

As you walk upon the earth plane fully activated with these new Holy Grail light codes, you shall imprint the energy of peace and love into the earth.

Today, as you accept this beautiful gift, may you open your heart to the energy of Grace Elohim. Allow her essence to merge with your own soul as you feel her love and peace. Accept this gift with an open heart for it is time for you to receive.

What a beautiful gift that you have given to yourselves and to the world as you receive these powerful Holy Grail light codes. You are all the new earth beings embodying these powerful codes within your essence, for indeed, you are the change you wish to see for you are assisting Mother Gaia and all of humanity to return to love and to be at peace.

Go now, my children. Feel the glory of these powerful healing codes as you merge in consciousness with the energy of All That Is. Go now, my children. Be at peace. Be at peace. Be at peace. And so it is.

Ascended Master Sarah

Lea Chapin

Chapter 13

Invoking the Diamond Light to Return to Sacred Union

Greetings, dear ones, it is I, Sarah. This is a powerful time of inner transformation and spiritual awakening. I come to reactivate the Holy Grail light codes into all of humanity so that every soul's Diamond Light Body may embody the Supreme Creator's pure essence of love and light.

I am excited to share that many souls are allowing their beautiful Diamond Light Bodies to be reactivated once again into their full divine potential. Dear ones, your Diamond Light Body is being reawakened by the new Holy Grail light codes as you embody the Sophia/Christ Consciousness.

This upgrade in consciousness is a part of the new earth timeline as humanity awakens into the Seventh Golden Age of Enlightenment. As humanity ascends in consciousness, the energy of Mother Earth will continue in her own ascension process into the fifth dimensional frequency.

May I explain the meaning of ascension as the word ascension has been most confusing for many lightworkers. Ascension is not about being taken off the planet into another dimensional frequency or being magically transported into the higher realms of light. Ascension essentially is awakening and embodying one's spiritual divinity here on earth.

It is about fully embodying your true spiritual divine potential as you merge with your I Am presence. As the energy on earth continues to be upgraded with the new Holy Grail light codes, the purification of these powerful frequencies are causing chaos in the world.

It is causing an unraveling of the old paradigm and structures of the old patriarchal world of control and dominance that can no longer be held within the collective consciousness of humanity. The planet and humanity are in a powerful purification process that is affecting many humans physically, mentally, emotionally, and energetically.

As Mother Gaia raises her vibrational frequency, many souls are unable to handle these powerful energies and are unable to cope with their own emotions. The increase in violence, road rage, mass shooting, and explosive behaviors of rage and anger are a part of these new frequencies that are affecting so many.

Mother Gaia is undergoing a powerful purification process as well. The erratic weather patterns and earth changes that are occurring are also a part of this transformational process and purification of lower vibrational frequencies upon the planet. Mother Gaia is being rewired and upgraded to be able to stabilize herself as the new Holy Grail light codes emerge upon the planet.

The entire solar system is busy recalibrating these higher frequencies as Mother Gaia is in the midst of a spiritual evolution as she transitions from the third dimensional frequency into the fifth dimensional frequency of light.

I, Sarah, am here to anchor the energies of the Holy Grail light codes into the planet in order to help maintain balance on the planet during this great time of purification. During this Great Awakening. Your higher self is merging into Sacred Union with your I Am presence as you become fully actualized and empowered into your true divine potential.

As you awaken to your I Am presence, your Diamond Light Body can now begin to receive these powerful frequencies as you merge into your Crystalline Light Body. The function of the Diamond Light Body is to bring balance to your energetic field that will allow you to hold more light and love within your physicality and into all aspects of your being.

The Holy Grail light codes can be described as various geometric shapes, each having specific colors and varied impacts on the energy templates of the body. The Diamond Light Body is a grid of golden white light that surrounds and penetrates the physical body and the etheric field.

This grid is comprised of electrical magnetic frequencies that are extremely potent and powerful. The diamond light grid is a conduit to access the higher spiritual frequencies that are being emitted by the Holy Grail codes.

Dear ones, I ask you to imagine yourselves as the beautiful diamond light that you are, sparkling in your magnificence and your brilliance. Can you feel your Diamond Light Body shining so that others may feel your energy and see your magnificence?

Your Diamond Light Body is a part of your Merkabic field, and it holds and carries your signature vibration of love, peace and light. Allow yourselves to receive this gift that I bring to you as I infuse the Holy Grail light codes into your Diamond Light Body. It is an exciting time to be on the planet as you merge in consciousness with the Sophia/Christ Consciousness.

Dear children, you have come to this planet to assist during this powerful ascension, and you have done this many times before in other planets, solar systems, and galaxies. You have volunteered to serve Mother Gaia during her ascension process in this new Seventh Golden Age of Enlightenment.

Please allow yourselves to receive these new Holy Grail light codes as you merge into your beautiful Diamond Light Body so that you may continue to serve Mother Gaia.

Dear ones, I ask you to release any lower vibrational frequencies of fear, anger, hatred that may interfere with the activation of the new light codes that are being reactivated within you.

So please, take a deep breath, and release all that no longer serves you. As a powerful spirit, you are able to master your own emotions and thought forms as you raise your frequency into the higher vibrational frequencies of love and peace.

Dear ones, I hear your cries for help during this great purification process. What is my purpose? What am I doing on this planet? Why is there so much chaos, confusion and violence? Why is it so difficult to live on this earth plane? Will there ever be peace on earth?

I hear your cries for help and understand your concerns are real and valid. I tell you, dear ones, that this purification is necessary as it is part of the birthing process into the new Golden Age. I ask you to be patient with yourselves, be patient with the world, knowing that everything truly is in divine order.

Allow yourselves to trust that there is a divine plan for this planet and all of humanity during this powerful ascension period.

It is why I am coming to help accelerate your consciousness into the higher dimensional frequencies so that you may have a greater understanding of your soul purpose on this planet. As the Holy Grail light codes activate your Diamond Light Body, you shall begin to feel a sense of personal empowerment as you awaken to your I Am presence.

As you awaken your higher self will guide you into a clear vision of your soul pathway and soul purpose. As you grow stronger in your connection to your higher self, you will be able to attract greater abundance in all areas of your life. As you merge with your Diamond Light Body you are able to obtain self-mastery.

Remember, dearest children, that you are here on this planet as you have chosen to serve during this powerful ascension period. Today, as you allow me to bring these Holy Grail codes within your essence, may you feel the power of your own spirit as you return to Oneness and live in Holy Divine Sacred Union with all of life.

Please receive God's love and light as you prepare yourselves for the greatest assignment of your lives.

Go now, my children, as you receive the new Holy Grail codes within your essence, go forth in the love, the light from which you were created as a magnificent physical spiritual being of light that has come to serve and to be served. And so it is.

Ascended Master Sarah

Chapter 14

Return
to Sacred Divine Union

Greetings, dear ones, it is I, Sarah. It is my honor to assist humanity to merge in Divine Sacred Union with the Sacred Feminine and Sacred Masculine energies that are your birthright. Today I ask your permission to invoke the Holy Grail light codes into your essence for the integration of the Divine Masculine, Divine Feminine essences to be brought forth into your being.

In preparation for the integration of these energies, please take a deep breath and breathe in the energy and the essence of Father-Mother-God as one unified force field of light. The blending of the Sacred Masculine and Sacred Feminine energies is the journey home to integration into Divine Holy Sacred Union.

You, dear ones, are all new earth beings that are being reintegrated and reactivated with the Holy Grail light codes that are now healing the planet. As I bring the recalibration of these frequencies within your essence, may you open your hearts to receive the power of God's love as you merge into Divine Holy Sacred Union with All That Is.

As you receive this integration, may you visualize a large diamond within you. It is called your Crystalline Diamond Light Field. It is in the shape of a pyramid that joins at your pelvic region. It extends one foot above your head and one foot below your feet, and it extends approximately two feet out on both sides of your body.

Visualize yourself directly in the center of this beautiful Diamond Light Field as your spine is aligned with the center of the diamond light. May I invoke the Holy Grail light codes into your light body so you may merge with your Diamond Light Field?

The first Holy Grail light code is the beautiful Violet Ray that will merge with your Diamond Light Body. The violet light ranges from a deep purple to pale lilac and all shades in between as it penetrates deep into the cells and tissues of your physical body.

Breathe in the color violet as you allow this ray to enter in from your crown chakra, merging with all of your chakras. Please allow the color violet to enter into your earth star chakra. As it penetrates into the crystalline core of Mother Earth, the new earth Holy Grail codes are also being infused into the core of Mother Earth as well.

Now I ask you to take another deep breath and allow me to invoke the Yellow Ray of light into your Diamond Light Body. Breathe in the color yellow as you allow this ray to enter in from your crown chakra, merging with all of your chakras.

Please allow the color yellow to enter into your earth star chakra. As it penetrates into the crystalline core of

Mother Earth the new earth Grail codes are also being infused into the core of Mother Earth as well.

Now, beloved ones, I ask you to breathe in the energy of the Copper Ray. Breathe in the energy of the Copper Ray within your crown chakra as it merges with all of your chakras as you connect to your earth star chakra, as you connect to the crystalline core of Mother Gaia. So breathe in the energy of the Copper Ray as you feel this energy healing your soul.

Dear ones, I ask you to breathe in the energy of the Golden White ray, allowing your heart to open to this beautiful frequency of peace, tranquility and love. Breathe in the Golden White Ray as you merge this frequency into your heart chakra, as your heart begins to expand even further into cosmic love.

Allow the energy of the Golden White Ray to merge into all your chakras as it once again reconnects to your earth star chakra and into the crystalline core of Mother Earth.

May you lovingly receive these new Holy Grail light codes into your being as you merge into Divine Holy Sacred Union with All That Is.

Dear ones, I now ask you to breathe in the energy of the Silver Ray, the beautiful ray of wisdom and remembrance. As you call in the frequency of the Silver Ray, you will begin to stimulate your pineal gland to awaken to your innate wisdom.

So please breathe in the Silver Ray, breathing this powerful frequency as you once again connect it to all your chakras and into the earth star chakra as you connect into the crystalline core of Mother Gaia.

Beloved souls, call in the energy of the Blue Ray. As you breathe the Blue Ray into your heart chakra, allow the

Blue Ray to connect to all your chakras as you once again connect to the earth star chakra and into the crystalline core of Mother Gaia. Breathe in the Blue Ray as it shall bring compassion, peace, tranquility and mercy into your own soul.

Dear ones, breathe in the Pink Ray, the energy of cosmic love. Breathe in the Pink Ray as you embody this frequency in Divine Holy Sacred Union within your essence. As you breathe in the Pink Ray, allow it to merge with all your chakras, once again connecting to the earth star charka and into the crystalline core of Mother Gaia.

Feel the energy of the Pink Ray of divine cosmic love as it sends healing and peace into the heart of Mother Gaia.

Beloved souls it is my honor to introduce you to the energy of the Pearlescent White Ray of purity, innocence and love. This is my signature vibration as it holds and carries my essence. It is a powerful frequency that is being emitted on this planet to help assist humanity to return to balance and to live in Divine Holy Sacred Union with all of life.

Please breathe in the Pearlescent White Ray as you allow it to enter into all your chakras, once again connecting to the earth star chakra and into the crystalline core of Mother Gaia. The Pearlescent White Ray is the original energy in which your spirit was created. Can you feel the power of your spirit as you breathe in the Pearlescent White Ray? Can you feel your divine spark reignited once again?

Dear ones, can you feel the energy of these powerful Holy Grail light codes reactivating and recalibrating within your system? Can you feel the light codes fortifying the Divine Masculine and Divine Feminine aspects within your being as you merge into Sacred Divine Union with your I Am presence? As you reunify within your sacred Divine Self, we call it the Sacred Dance, the Sacred Dance of your spirit.

It is the balance of the two aspects of the male-female polarities. You have now come home to yourselves and have reawakened once again to the Sacred Dance of your true spirit essence.

Dearest children, I ask you to receive these beautiful light rays as you open your hearts to feel the energy of purity, innocence and love once again. May you receive these frequencies as a gift for your dedication and commitment to serving Mother Gaia as an earth volunteer.

May your hearts receive my love from the Pearlescent White Ray. May you return to love and be at peace.

Go now, my children. Prepare yourselves to receive. Prepare yourselves to receive. Prepare yourselves to receive. Go in peace. Go in peace. Go in peace. And so it is.

Ascended Master Sarah

Chapter 15

Sarah Anchors the Integration of Divine Sacred Union Within Your Being

Greetings, dear ones, it is I, Sarah. It is my honor to anchor the energy of Divine Holy Sacred Union within your beings. May you receive the balance of Divine Masculine and Divine Feminine energies once again into your souls so that you may embody the energy of the Sacred Dance of your Spirit.

Dear ones, this is of great importance in order for peace to prevail upon the planet. Today, as you receive this integration of the balanced Sacred Feminine and Masculine energies within your essence, please allow yourselves to feel the energy and the essence of my love for you.

I come as the representation of the missing Holy Grail bringing the new Holy Grail light codes and my Pearlescent White Flame of purity, innocence and love for all to receive. I welcome you into the family of light as new earth beings fully embodied into the Sophia/Christ Consciousness of Divine Holy Sacred Union.

Today you are also being graced by Grace Elohim. Her essence and her frequency is here to help you return to balance and to be at peace. Allow her to open your heart chakra so you may remember the true essence of your powerful spirit. As you awaken your divine Essent self, your true sacred soul mission shall come forth.

As Grace Elohim and I help to lift the veils of forgetfulness from your consciousness, may you re-remember the power of your divine self. It is my honor to bring the Pearlescent White Flame of purity, love and innocence onto the planet so that all souls may re-remember their sacred soul mission.

As you integrate and receive the Pearlescent White Flame into your being, may you feel the peace and the love that you so long for. Grace Elohim and I wish to share our love with you so that you may feel the power of your own spirit's purity, innocence, and grace. Dear ones, breathe in our love as we heal your souls with the Pearlescent White Flame of Purification as you return to Oneness.

Today is a completion day as you return to partner and union with your divine self. Once again, dear ones, allow yourselves to reclaim the divinity of your divine spirit. I remember Union. I remember Union. You have now come home to yourselves as you live in joy and remembrance of who you truly are.

Beloved souls, breathe in the Pearlescent White Flame that is being emitted upon this planet for all to receive and to embody. This flame is being ignited onto the earth at this time as a symbol of Divine Holy Sacred Union with All That Is. It is the essence that my parents, Yeshua and

Mary Magdalene, left as an imprint for future generations to receive. It is my privilege to share their essence and the energy of the Pearlescent White Flame of Divine Holy Sacred Union for all to receive.

Dear ones, please breathe in the Pearlescent White Flame to clear all that no longer serves you so that you may ascend in consciousness with your divine self. Allow the Pearlescent White Flame of purity, innocence and love to fill every cell, every fiber, every pore of your being with love, light and peace. May you feel the joy in remembrance of who you truly are as a divine child of light.

May you awaken to your true sacred mission as you return to Oneness and embody the greater wisdom of your divine spirit. As you allow yourselves to receive this beautiful gift, may your heart open to cosmic love, peace and grace.

As the Pearlescent White Ray is activated within your being, allow your cellular memory to once again re-remember how you once lived in peace. As lightworkers, you are all messengers of hope, inspiration, love and peace for Mother Earth. You all are holding the balance for Mother Earth to ascend into the fifth dimensional frequency and beyond.

May you feel the power of your spirit as you merge into Oneness with your divine Essent self. As you open yourselves to receive the love that I bring to you, allow your hearts to open to the truth of who you are. You have come home to yourselves as you have returned to Oneness. May you be at peace.

It is my honor to be the voice and the oracle of the missing Holy Grail for I am the missing chalice that so many are seeking. Dear ones, the chalice is no longer missing for it is inside of each of you. May the energy of the Pearlescent White Flame awaken your remembrance that you are a child of God.

The Pearlescent White Flame is awakening all souls to cosmic love, peace and grace which they have been seeking for so long. Remember, the search no longer continues for the search is inside of yourself.

I thank you for allowing me to bring my inspirational messages through the course of these teachings to help awaken you to the remembrance of who you truly are. Each of you are a gift to the world and indeed you are the change you wish to see.

As you hold and carry the living light of God's pure essence within your souls, you shall become the peacekeepers and the way showers for this new Golden Age of Enlightenment.

As I leave you now with the lyrics of John Lennon's song, "Imagine," may you feel the power of his love as he has gifted these beautiful lyrics for all to receive.

IMAGINE

(lyrics from "Imagine: John Lennon" soundtrack)

Imagine there's no heaven
It's easy if you try
No hell below us
Above us only sky
Imagine all the people
Living for today...Aha-ah...

Imagine there's no countries
It isn't hard to do
Nothing to kill or die for
And no religion, too
Imagine all the people
Living life in peace...You...

You may say I'm a dreamer
But I'm not the only one
I hope someday you'll join us
And the world will be as one

Imagine no possessions
I wonder if you can
No need for greed or hunger
A brotherhood of man
Imagine all the people
Sharing all the world... You...

You may say I'm a dreamer
But I'm not the only one

I hope someday you'll join us
And the world will live as one"

Imagine a world filled with peace. It begins with one soul at a time. Beloved ones, allow yourselves to receive. Go in peace.

Sarah, Goddess of Peace,
Daughter of Yeshua and Mary Magdalene

Introduction
to the Twelve Tools of Enlightenment
Narrated by Mary Magdalene

As you may already know, the beautiful Sacred Feminine energy has begun to emerge stronger upon your planet. This is due, in part, because many souls have opened their heart chakras to the Sacred Feminine with the power of her love and compassion.

These attributes are so needed to heal your planet and the hearts of all who have lived in fear and separation from God. We ask you to re-remember the truth that you are powerful spiritual beings of light. You carry the balance of the Father-Mother-God essence within you as you are all here to share your love with the world.

So many of you are searching outside yourselves for love, it is through your connection to your own innate wisdom and inner gnosis that you shall begin to feel more empowered in your own soul. You were all born with the gift of gnosis and inner gnosis, but over time separated yourselves from your own knowing and your own inner truth.

You became separated from your own I Am presence, and this is when separation, darkness and fear set in the collective human consciousness. It was Yeshua and my sacred soul contract to help guide humanity to rediscover the truth of who you truly are as divine beings of light connected to All That Is.

Sacred Union and Sacred Balance comes by listening to the inner still quiet voice of God that lives inside each of us. Dear ones, we are here to teach you that it is as simple as connecting to your breath.

This is why Yeshua has brought forth the Twelve Tools of Enlightenment to teach you how to connect to your I Am presence through the breath. It is through your breath that you shall connect to God and return to balance and be at peace that you so long for.

Dear ones, the Twelve Tools of Enlightenment will help you begin to quiet your mind and energetically align yourself to the God essence. It is here within God's essence that miracles abound.

Through the light and the love that you hold, all the beautiful gifts that you are here to bring unto the world can be made manifest. I ask you to open your beautiful heart chakra and allow yourself to receive the power of the Twelve Tools of Enlightenment. These are the keys of enlightenment that will help you to unlock the doors to all that you seek.

Transmission from Mary Magdalene

The Twelve Tools of Enlightenment
Narrated by:
Yeshua (Jesus the Christ)

Greetings, my Beloveds, it is I, Yeshua. As I enter into your vibration, I bow to each of you. I ask you to hold your frequency and vibration to the highest level you're possibly able to embody. With the new energy of this powerful paradigm shift, each of you are to live as sacred beings.

The energy of Mother Earth has shifted so beautifully, so powerfully, and so exponentially that each of you have grown and expanded more than you can truly understand. Today, as I help each of you use what I call your box of tools, I ask you to feel this freedom and joy and to truly live in the essence of love.

May I begin by explaining my first tool? My first tool is the breath of life. The beautiful energy and essence of the breath of life connects you instantly to the seventh dimensional frequency. As you allow your body to breathe and expand, it will hold the essence and the power of the beautiful life force and energy of God.

As you hold the frequency of the vital life force of the God essence within your breath, begin to relax, surrender, and let go and let God. It is unfortunate many humans are not able to breathe fully due to anxiety, fear, or stress. Shallow breathing cuts you off from the light source of God's energy.

As you breathe, please align yourself to connect to the Living Light of God. And breathe, truly allow yourself to breathe. When you fully breathe, you align yourself to your higher self, you align yourself to the power of the light. To the energy of the Prana that lies deep inside of your being. And so breathe, Dearest Ones. Breathe.

My second tool is the third eye. Your second tool, Dear Ones, allows you to move into a state of awareness. Focus your attention on your third eye. God has gifted you with this beautiful energy of sight, with clairvoyance. It is there, between your brows, that your third eye resides.

It is connected to your pineal gland, where all the ancient teachings are held. All that you have ever been, and all that you shall ever become, is held in the pineal gland. So breathe, Dearest Children, breathe in the energy of the white light of God into your third eye. Breathe into your pineal gland and allow your vessel to open to the awareness of All That Is. So breathe into your third eye.

As we move into the third tool, focus on opening your heart chakra. There within your sacred heart, you hold love for yourself. Allow your beautiful sacred heart to open like a beautiful lotus flower. Your sacred heart holds the purity and innocence of your soul. Breathe, Dear Children, and allow your heart to open and awaken, like a beautiful lotus flower.

See your beautiful sacred heart opening and know that you are a pure vessel of love. Breathe into your sacred heart with intention. As you open the energy of the sacred heart, I ask that you awaken your high heart. It is located in the center of your physical back, behind your physical heart. It is different from your sacred and merciful heart; it is a beautiful energy that is connected to All That Is. So breathe, Dearest Children, into your high heart with intention.

May we move to the fourth tool of your high heart? As you transition to the fourth tool, allow yourself to move into the high heart. It is within your high heart that you connect to love. As you connect through your breath, allow yourself to feel the energy of pure love, and pure understanding, that we are all connected, and we are all One. As you expand into the dimensions of all that you've ever been, and all that you shall ever become, allow yourself to expand into your high heart.

Breathe with the intention of opening your heart to Oneness, opening your beautiful heart, and feel the love multidimensionally, on all levels, and within all aspects of your being. And so breathe into your high heart. Breathe, my Children, breathe.

Now we move into the fifth tool, your sacred belly. So breathe, Dearest Ones, and allow the beautiful sacred belly to open. Begin to breathe the energy within your sacred belly, opening the expansion of the pure white light frequency within your sacred belly.

Allowing the energy of this powerful essence, of all of creation, to begin to move through you. It is through your breath that you form the energy of creation. Buddha, the laughing Buddha, held the energy of laughter in his sacred belly.

Why is Buddha represented with a big belly and laughter? He knew and understood the power of the sacred belly, he understood the power of laughter. For it is the secret to the creative life force energy. So breathe, Dearest Children, breathe into your sacred belly. Breathe into the sacred center that awakens your kundalini. It awakens all your cells, and the beautiful essence of your Merkabic lightbody.

So laugh and breathe, and hold your sacred belly to feel joy, laughter, freedom, and peace. So breathe, my Children, breathe, and allow yourself to feel the energy of creative life force essence. Breathe into this beautiful expanding energy as you connect to the Oneness and feel laughter and joy in your sacred belly.

Now we move to the sixth tool, the energy within your sacrum. Here the kundalini rises from your sacrum and your coccyx into your spine. This is your sacred holding point that connects you to your physicality and to Mother Earth. Feel the essence of this beautiful energy of your sacrum, feel the beautiful energy of Mother Earth, and breathe in this energy through your sacrum.

Breathe and release, breathe and release, breathe and release. For many, their sacrum has been stuck, and they have not allowed the vital life force energy of Mother Earth to move through them. And so, Dearest Children, open your sacrum.

You are no longer stuck, you are free. It is here, as you begin to allow your kundalini to rise, that the Pranic life force energy moves through you. And so breathe with intention, Dearest Ones, breathe with the intention that you are free, breathe with the intention that you are free. Breathe and release and open your sacral heart and set yourself free.

Now we move into our seventh tool, the sacred star point. As we go into the seventh tool, allow yourself to move the energy from this beautiful sacred star point. The star points are powerful energy points behind your physical knees that hold you and ground you to the Earth. Open this beautiful energy by bringing in the star point through your breath, for it is a gateway into your physicality, between you and Mother Earth.

As you move this energy from Mother Earth in through the star point, it will allow you to be able to move forward into your life mission. Do you choose to move forward in your mission? If you do, then breathe, breathe in the sacred star point. Breathe in the life essence of Mother Earth into your body.

Breathe into this powerful vortex of energy that's held behind your physical knees. It truly is the energy that is grounding you into this third dimension, but it also allows you to hold the sacred energy of Mother Earth. So breathe with intention into your high heart, into your sacred star point, and breathe.

So now, we move into the eighth tool, the Earth star. As you move into this eighth tool, it is within the very soles of your physical feet that you feel this powerful energy of the Earth star. This energy connects you on a very deep level to Mother Earth, and so, breathe, Dearest Children, and call in this energy of the Earth star, and open the Earth star which is in the soles of your feet to connect through your breath.

Breathe with intention and open to this beautiful portal. It is time to allow yourself to stay connected to Mother Earth on all levels, in your physicality, in your mental, emotional, and all aspects of your being. It is necessary during this paradigm shift that each of you stay connected to Mother Earth and stay present within your body.

And so breathe, Dearest Children, this is the power of the Earth star. The new energy on the planet is extremely powerful, and because of the paradigm shift, many will not be able to hold the energy of the new frequencies if they do not stay connected to the Earth star, to Mother Gaia, so breathe into the Earth star.

Understand Mother Earth is now opening and expanding as a beautiful star of love and light and peace. So breathe into her essence and feel the energy through the soles of your feet, breathe in the beautiful Earth star, so that you too may ascend as a sacred being of light, as Mother Earth ascends.

Now we move into the ninth tool, the Divine Mother energy, the portal of entry. As you go into the ninth tool, I ask you to breathe with intention, and move into the crystalline grid of Mother Earth, of the Goddess energy, of Mother Gaia's energy. This is not the crystalline core of Mother Earth, but it is a portal, an opening, a gateway to the energy of the Divine Feminine.

As you enter into this gateway, feel the unconditional love, peace, joy, and compassion there. And so breathe, my Children, breathe. As you deeply feel this connection to the energies of the Earth Mother and the Divine Mother, understand that it is a beautiful gateway; it is the divine portal to Mother Gaia, known as the Divine Feminine.

When you first chose to come here, you entered into this powerful portal of the Divine Feminine and asked her permission to enter the Earth plane. Mother Gaia welcomed you as the beautiful Starseed you are. She acknowledges your beautiful spirit and welcomes you home once again.

So breathe in this loving energy of the Divine Feminine of Mother Gaia and honor the knowing that she resides within your physical essence. So breathe in her energy with intention.

Now we move into the tenth tool, the portal of peace. I ask that you allow yourself to feel this connection to the portal of peace. You are a powerful being of light who chose to be here in this paradigm shift, during this new age of enlightenment. You chose to be here to assist the planet at this time.

I ask you to move deeper into the energy of Mother Gaia, into the portal of peace, which is the next level beyond the portal of entry. The peace portal is felt and held in the sixth dimension frequency, breathe and open to this energy through your Earth star point. And move into Mother Gaia's portal of entry of her peace portal.

Breathe, my Children, breathe with intention. This portal is a holding station, and as each of you were held in this portal of peace before you entered into your physicality on this Earth plane, your entire being was embodied with peace. There within this beautiful portal, you were able to breathe with intention, as you entered into the Earth plane.

I ask you to once again breathe and move into the portal of peace. It is the essence of who you are, it is the essence of Mother Gaia, it is why you came to be on this Earth plane. Today, I, Yeshua, come to you to help you to move into this beautiful portal. It is time now for you to activate this portal, as each of you are physical portals of peace.

Breathe with intention into your own portal, breathe in the gateway of Mother Gaia's peace portal, the Divine Feminine portal for Mother Earth. You entered into this

Earth plane as joyful and peaceful spirits. Please breathe in this energy with intention, so Mother Earth may return back to the planet of peace, love, and joy in which she was created.

We move now into the eleventh tool, the silver ray, the eleventh tool of our new paradigm shift into the new age of enlightenment for the new Earth. It connects you to the beautiful essence of the silver ray, of the silver star. May you understand that we all have a silver cord that connects us to our higher self and keeps us grounded to the Earth plane.

When we all transition from our physical bodies, the silver cord is disbanded, and we ascend back into our true spirit form. The silver ray allows you to merge into the essence of all that you are, and through all multi-dimensional levels of time and space. Breathe, my Children, breathe in the energy of the silver ray with intention.

It truly is your life force energy and essence. It is the energy of All That Is, it is the energy of the Great Creator. As it holds and connects you to the beautiful energy of Mother Earth, the silver ray is truly your lifeline. Breathe it in with intention, as this energy is the peace portal that is held inside your being.

And finally, we move to the twelfth tool, the energy of Oneness. Breathe with intention the energy of Oneness as you expand your essence into the beautiful white light energy of God. You will feel the power of God's white light surrounding you, embracing you, protecting you, encompassing you, as you are the white light.

Remember, Dearest Children, there is no time, there is no space, there is no separation, there is only Oneness. You are light, you are love. You are not just an individual in a physical body, you are a beautiful spirit of light connected to the energy and essence of All That Is.

So breathe in the essence of this beautiful white light and simply allow yourself to feel the essence and presence of peace, through every fiber of your being. Breathe, my Children.

Breathe in the essence of the white light of God. Breathe in your Oneness. Breathe in the silver ray, the silver star which grounds you into the energy of Mother Gaia.

As you move through the peace portal of the white light of God, allow yourself to move into the portal of Mother Earth, the Divine portal, which is a beautiful gateway of unconditional love, peace, joy, Oneness, harmony, and balance.

Breathe in the energy into your soul, breathe it into your physicality, and move yourself into your sacred Earth star with intention. Then move into your sacred star point with intention. And then move into your sacrum with freedom, and joy, with intention. Then move into your sacred belly with laughter, joy, and intention.

Then move into your high heart with love and gratitude and intention. Then move into your sacred and merciful heart with compassion and mercy, with intention. Then move into your third eye with knowingness and clarity, with intention.

Finally, Dearest Ones, breathe and move the breath of life into your pineal gland. This holds your ancient wisdom and is the connection to All That Is.

I ask you, Dearest Children, to hold the essences of these twelve tools. When you feel nervous, fearful, or alone, I ask you to use these tools to calm yourself. May your heart awaken to the essence and the presence of these tools. May you feel the light and love of God surrounding you.

As you choose to be the light of the world, remember to be the change that you wish to see. So breathe in these new paradigm frequencies, breathe in these new portals of light, into your physicality, into all aspects of your being. Dearest Ones, you are the light, the way, and the truth.

For you have known and have understood that you are pure love, you are pure light, you are the essence of the energy of All There Is. May you be at peace as you allow these beautiful tools to open you to the frequency of who you truly are, which is a divine spirit. Remember to always let your light shine so that others may see. Go in peace.

Yeshua (Jesus the Christ)

The Twelve Tools of Enlightenment from both Mary Magdalene and Yeshua can also be found on Lea's website in CD and MP3 form to further enhance activation of the twelve tools.

Afterword

By Lea Chapin

It has been an honor and a privilege to be an oracle for the Holy Family. As of this writing, I have dedicated over 29 years of my life as a direct voice channel for Spirit bringing inspirational messages to the world to help humanity awaken and ascend into this new Golden Age of Enlightenment.

It all began on March 21, 1993, when I was receiving a Reiki healing session and I spontaneously began to hear my spiritual guide, Grand, speak to me telepathically. At that time in my life I had never had such an experience, so I was deeply shocked and surprised by this most unusual spiritual phenomenon.

Because I was curious by nature and an avid spiritual seeker of higher wisdom teachings, I began my daily practice of connecting to Grand through channeled communication.

Those early years were very exciting to me as I was growing spiritually with each passing day. I was like a sponge. I wanted to connect and grow closer to God and enlighten my soul with as much spiritual wisdom as I could receive and absorb.

Over the next four years I worked exclusively with Grand. Then the most remarkable and unimaginable experience happened; I began to receive inspirational messages from Yeshua, Mother Mary, Mary Magdalene, and the Holy Family. I was once again in shock for I did not understand why I was receiving the messages at that time.

I remember questioning myself. Why are they speaking to me? I had no specific religious training, nor was I affiliated with any religious doctrine. I considered myself a spiritual student of metaphysics and I believed in God, but I was not religious. Why were these great beings coming to me?

It wasn't long before I came to understand my role as their oracle. They explained to me that during their lifetime I had been Mother Mary's niece and Yeshua's cousin, Elizabeth. I soon began to have visions of my life as Elizabeth, living with the Holy Family over 2,000 years ago.

I slowly began to accept who I was and the role that I played in that lifetime. I could feel Elizabeth's essence come alive within me. I could sense her strength, wisdom and tenacity. I could also relate to her gentle sweet nature, as well as the determination she had to accomplish whatever she set her mind to.

She was called the "task master" and I could feel her intensity, strength and devotion to Yeshua's mission. I could literally feel Elizabeth and me becoming one.

After many years went by, I was instructed by Yeshua in 2003 that I was to dictate my first book with him. The message he gave during this dictation represented the true essence of Christ's teachings. This book became <u>The Twelve Mastery Teachings of Christ</u>, published in 2005.

Then, as Christ would have it, he came to me again and asked me to write the book about his life with Mary Magdalene and their love story as Twin Flames. Initially I balked at the idea for I was afraid of being ridiculed for bringing such a controversial story line out into the world.

But I trusted Yeshua, so I went ahead with the project. For me, writing this book had been painful and joyous. I started and stopped this process for over three years but something inside me pushed me to complete the book. I knew that despite my own fears I had to honor my sacred soul contrast just as Elizabeth did during her lifetime.

So I persisted, and now in this lifetime, a part of my sacred soul contract had been fulfilled by writing the love story of Yeshua and Mary Magdalene. I am proud to be their oracle and am honored to share their story and their life with the entire world.

I received such positive feedback from so many around the world after I published <u>Divine Union: The Love Story of Jesus and Mary Magdalene</u> my fears have been reconciled. I am proud to share this beautiful love story that was brought forth through their own words.

So now I have been called to bring forth the teachings of Sarah, Yeshua's and Mary Magdalene's daughter, entitled <u>Sacred Wisdom Teachings of Sarah, Goddess of Peace</u>.

Ascended Master Sarah brings forth the path of the integration and transformation of the balance of Divine Feminine and Divine Masculine aspects that is so needed upon this planet at this time. As their daughter, she carries the combined energies of their Sacred Union within her own DNA and is known as the living Holy Grail.

She is here as the trinity, holding the frequency of their conjoined energies as she embodies the energy of Divine Oneness and is the representation of the missing chalice. Her story is the continuation of Jesus and Mary Magdalene's love story, <u>Divine Union: The Love Story of Jesus and Mary Magdalene</u>.

I invite you to journey into the heart of her wisdom teachings as she is here to help you discover the secrets of the missing grail that shall unite you in Sacred Union with your Divine Self.

Goddess of Peace: Sacred Wisdom Teachings of Ascended Master Sarah

Ascended Master Sarah carries the Holy Grail Light Codes of her parents. As told in Divine Union: The Love Story of Jesus and Mary Magdalene, Sarah shares her mother's wisdom teachings of The Way of the Chalice to restore balance, love, peace and unity consciousness upon the planet.

Through Sarah's wisdom teachings, we gain the insight to overcome the deeply rooted imbalanced masculine and feminine energies that have created chaos that is so prevalent upon the planet.

Sarah's wisdom teachings lead us back to Sacred Union of integration, wholeness and Oneness, which is the true path of enlightenment and self-mastery.

Goddess of Peace, Sacred Wisdom Teachings of Ascended Master Sarah leads us on a journey to discover the truth of the missing Holy Grail that so many have been seeking since the Last Supper.

Lea Chapin, M.S. Ed., B.S. Psychology, is an educator, psychotherapist, spiritual counselor and medium. In 1993, Lea began receiving divinely inspired messages from Spirit when her gifts of clairaudience, clairvoyance, and clairsentience allowed her access to the true teachings of the Ascended Masters and Angelic Realm as a versatile direct voice channel for Spirit.

Her life is now devoted to spiritual pursuits and empowering all who choose to reawaken to their own Sacred Balance and divinity.

Lea has a Bachelor's Degree in Psychology and has a Master's Degree in Counselor Education. She has over 40 years of experience as both a psychotherapist and an inspirational spiritual counselor.

Lea is able to receive divinely inspired, spiritually channeled information from the Ascended Masters and spiritual realm to assist her clients with a renewed perspective of their current life issues and challenges. She has coined the tagline "Practical Spirituality for Real Life Solutions."

Currently Lea conducts private counseling sessions as well as educational workshops and inspirational seminars, both as a teacher and motivational speaker.

In 1993, Lea began to receive divinely inspired messages from Spirit when her gifts of clairaudience, clairvoyance, clairsentience and claircognizance reawakened. This allowed her access to the teachings of the Ascended Masters and the Angelic Celestial Realms. She has been blessed to receive devotional and inspirational messages from Yeshua and Mary Magdalene and the Holy Family since 1997.

Her first book, <u>The Twelve Mastery Teachings of Christ</u>, was dictated directly from Yeshua in a series of twelve transmissions to explain the true essence of his teachings. Published in 2005, it is relevant today as the day it was received.

Her second book, <u>Divine Union: The Love Story of Jesus and Mary Magdalene</u>, was also written from direct transmissions from both Yeshua and Mary Magdalene. Each chapter is written as if they are speaking directly to us from their own voices about their lives as Twin Flames. Their love story had never been shared from their own deeply emotional perspective like this before, which makes this book quite unique. It was published in 2017.

Lea has devoted her life to the spiritual pursuit of raising the consciousness of humanity so peace may prevail upon this planet. She has also devoted her life to the teachings of the Holy Family, and she feels it is her spiritual mission to bring their messages to the world. She wishes to empower and enlighten all who wish to awaken to their own divinity.

She helps us remember that as our birthright, we are designed to live in peace, harmony, love and balance in order to live in joy and remembrance of who we truly are.

You can visit Lea's website at www.leachapin.com.

Made in the USA
Thornton, CO
08/30/23 17:04:45

59494be8-9f11-45ab-bb90-e7821403fd55R01